THE GOLDFISH EFFECT

UPGRADE YOUR MIND

ALEX ALEXANDER

ISBN: 979-8-3878-3600-8

Gratitude

I think gratitude is a place where intellect meets emotion—we feel good about the contributions others make to our lives, but we wouldn't feel anything without understanding the importance and generosity of their contributions.

I'm most grateful for my wife Ali, and my daughters, Kristen and Erin—the three most important people in my life, and the most joyful people I know. They set the context for everything about me...well, not everything, just the good stuff.

I'm grateful for the role Michael Gerber played in my life. He hired me in 1995, when I was a late blooming fifty-five year old. While working for him, I learned many important life lessons and turned my career in a direction that, at long last, provided deep satisfaction and a sense of contribution. Michael started out as my boss, quickly became a mentor, and ultimately became a friend.

Finally, I'm grateful for my Australian "brother" Don Farnden, who kept me in the game when I wanted to opt out. Don, even when overwhelmed with his own tribulations, was unfailingly supportive, and in truth, the driving force behind our business. He's one of the world's truly good blokes.

THE GOLDFISH EFFECT
Upgrade Your Mind

Table of Contents

Prelude: The Goldfish Effect

At the age of five, Brett asked his mother, "Can we put the goldfish in the bathtub?" So Ali poured Goldie from his small round bowl into the tub.

A strange thing happened. Despite the size of the tub, Goldie continued to swim in small circles exactly the size of his bowl.

It took a while, but Goldie learned that he could swim in bigger circles.

If you could talk with a goldfish about its life, it would be a short conversation, and it would go something like this:

You: *Hey, Goldie, what's the best thing about your life?*

Goldie: *It's my freedom—being able to do whatever I want whenever I want.*

You: *Are you really free?*

Goldie: *You bet I am. I can go up, down, left, right, in circles, or nowhere at all. I can eat my fish food whenever I want, and I can sleep whenever I want. I can talk to you or just shut up, and if I talk,*

> *I can say anything I want. I can do whatever I want whenever I want to do it or not do anything at all. If that's not free, I don't know what is.*

You: *Do you wish you could fly?*

Goldie: *What do you mean? I'm flying right now while I'm talking with you.*

You: *Do you wish you could get out of your bowl?*

Goldie: *What bowl? I have a whole universe to fly in. What more could there be?*

You: *Don't you wish you were more than just a goldfish?*

Goldie: *Hell no! What's better than being a goldfish?*

Metaphorically speaking, we're all goldfish, and we're enclosed within invisible bowls. The bowls are our unconscious minds.

Modern science of the mind proves time and again that our unconscious minds are responsible for 95 percent or more of our thinking, and for the most part, they control our lives. That's a good thing. If we had to think consciously about our every move and keep our memories in our conscious awareness...well, we just couldn't do it.

As miraculous as they are, our unconscious minds don't always serve us well. Unconscious habits of mind—especially the misleading ones known as cognitive biases—can, and often do, distort our thoughts and our sense of truth. Our flawed and biased habits of mind (everyone has them) are responsible for most of our mistakes and missteps, those times in our lives when we "go stupid."

Going stupid might sound somewhat insulting, but it accurately describes the mental mishaps and mistakes that arise from cognitive biases, bad habits of thinking, flawed mental models, emotionally driven behavior, unconscious illusions, and personality traits that sometimes make us behave badly. By and large, we humans are pretty intelligent creatures, but now and again, we all think, say, or do something that can only be described as stupid.

Most of us aren't aware that we're going stupid while it's happening. If we thought we were doing something stupid, we wouldn't do it. But because we're unaware, we go on about our lives, not recognizing our mistakes, believing ourselves to be rational, and convinced beyond doubt that we know what's true, what's right, what's ethical, and what's smart. We sometimes learn later that our words or actions were ill-advised, but in the moment—in real time—they seem right and justified.

The Goldfish Effect—the tendency of our unconscious minds to form habits that can make us go stupid—is insidious because we're unaware of it and what it could be doing to us. We don't know how or when our unconscious minds are leading us astray because the parts of our unconscious thinking that reach our conscious minds—the parts we're aware of—seem right, true, and rock solid, even when they're not. We see these mental lapses in others, but we almost never see them in ourselves. Not until we learn about them, and see them for what they are.

If you're open to the idea that your unconscious mind—your goldfish bowl—might sometimes cause you to go stupid, please read on even if you have serious doubts. If you're not open to this possibility, I wish you luck You'll need it.

Introduction

Going Stupid: It Happens to All of Us

Have you ever gone stupid? Yes, you have. So have I. I'm sorry if that sounds like an insult, but it's really not. It's entirely human and normal that even the smartest and sanest among us occasionally go stupid, some more than others, but we all do it.

If you doubt what I'm saying, take a moment to prove it for yourself. Look back at your own life and honestly answer a few questions.

Have you ever...

>...said something you didn't mean in the heat of the moment?

>...ignored facts or opinions or explained them away because they didn't agree with what you already believed?

>...made assumptions about someone or something based on appearances, a stereotype, or previous beliefs?

>...shouted at or used profanity on someone who didn't deserve it?

...blamed someone else when it was really your fault?

...trusted someone who had a nice face and seemed incredibly sincere, or mistrusted someone whose appearance made you uncomfortable?

...held back your own opinion because it would have been awkward or disruptive to disagree with everyone else?

...gone along with a bad decision rather than be the only one who didn't agree?

...behaved in a way that was inappropriate to the situation?

...let your emotions drive your behavior?

...jumped to a conclusion that later turned out wrong, then stuck to it anyway?

And scariest of all...

...have you ever made an important decision or taken a big risk, convinced at the time that it was the right thing to do, only to learn, sooner or later, that it was a lousy decision or a dangerous risk?

Going stupid is caused by mental biases and misperceptions, emotional overload, false beliefs (that we don't know are false), and even personality traits, all of which are inherent to the human mind. When our thinking is flawed—and it often is—it can cause us to believe things that aren't true, make questionable decisions, make mistakes that are avoidable, and see the world in distorted ways...all the while genuinely believing we're perfectly rational and thinking clearly.

Does it sound arrogant that I—someone who knows nothing about you—dare to assert that you have mental lapses that you don't know about? Well, first and foremost, it's not my claim. There is a rapidly growing body of scientific work—Nobel Prize-winning work—that makes the claim. I'm just the messenger. I'll tell you more about the science later.

A Shaky Foundation

Our brains, and therefore our minds, evolved to survive in a simpler world. Human evolution works over hundreds of thousands of years, but human progress happens in mere hundreds of years and, in modern times, only decades. The evolution of our brains hasn't been able to keep up.

We're managing our lives in a modern world with mental abilities evolved for a hunter-gatherer world of small tribes that were always in survival mode, coping with simple, stark conditions. But in the world of today, we have to deal with enormous communities made incomprehensible by technology. We're submerged in enormously complex societies, economies, ecologies, and belief systems. War used to be a stone axe affair. Food used to be a hunt-when-you're-hungry affair. Education used to be about learning how to hunt and forage, build a crude shelter, make rudimentary clothing, and not much more. Our brains evolved to deal with that, not with today's world.

Because evolution is slow but the modern world is changing quickly, we start our lives with brains that are behind the eight ball from the beginning, and then we muddle through our lives, careers, and relationships the best we can. For most of us, life is good or at least okay. But it's almost miraculous that we do as well as we do.

Most of the time, when we go stupid, the consequences are minor or unknown to us, and we make progress without knowing how much better it could be and without knowing when or how often we've gone stupid. No harm, no foul. But some of the time, we go stupid about important matters, and that can be devastating to our careers, our relationships, our health…anything we value.

We go stupid because of our habits of mind, which sometimes aren't appropriate for the situations we face in life. Inappropriate habits of mind affect everyone, yet, because these habits originate mostly in the unconscious mind, we're not aware of them. We suffer the consequences of going stupid, but we attribute our mistakes to anything but ourselves, believing without question that we are smart, and that something or someone else was the cause of the problem. We go stupid about politics, arguing with others who have gone stupid in a different direction. We go stupid about our relationships, thinking that our friends/partners/associates are the ones going stupid when it's really both of us. We go stupid about economics, climate change, race relations, gender issues, physical and mental health, and a long list of other matters—all of which are complex beyond human understanding. And we wonder why we're wrong so much of the time or, even worse, think ourselves smart and perceptive when we're anything but. We even go stupid about our own thoughts and beliefs, falling prey to unconscious biases and habits that tell us we're being smart when we're not.

Going stupid is not the same as being ignorant. Ignorance is merely a lack of information. Going stupid is the consequence of dysfunctional habits of mind. However the two reinforce each other—if you're ignorant about something and also mentally biased about it, it's a double whammy. But, as you'll see later, the more you overcome ignorance with learning, experience, and information—knowledge—the more that will help you build effective habits of mind and overcome the effects of dysfunctional ones. Knowledge isn't the cure for going stupid, but it's an important part of it.

There's an unseen problem inherent in all of this: everything we do, trivial or important, short or long term, depends on a shaky mental foundation. We start all of our important endeavors with minds that are subject to biases and mistakes, so we're always at risk of going stupid.

When our kids go to college, they do so with all their unconscious habits of mind in place, the useful ones as well as the dysfunctional ones. Unknown to them, they pile a college education on top of minds that evolved in a prehistoric world. If we want to start businesses, we define our entrepreneur's dream, put together a business plan, raise some seed money, and do it all under the influence of our unconscious habits of mind. When we want to get married and raise families, we go ahead, unaware of the many ways we might impair our relationships with our wives and kids because of our tendency to go stupid. Whatever we choose to do, however important or unimportant, we do it on top of a foundation that's susceptible to going stupid. Believing we're smart and wise, we manage our lives and careers, glibly unaware of the potential mischief lurking in our unconscious minds.

We need to become aware that we start everything from this shaky foundation, from inside our goldfish bowls. If we fix the foundation, everything that follows will be better: our careers, our relationships, our health…everything.

We Can Upgrade Our Minds

There's good news. There's a way to escape our goldfish bowls. We have the ability to adjust our minds, upgrade them, so to speak. We can learn about the ways our minds work, how they sometimes interfere with success and satisfaction, and then recondition ourselves to make them work better. Like the old Army advertising slogan used to say, we have a chance to be all we can be.

If you want to be the best version of you, you have to avoid or at least minimize the tendency to go stupid. When you're engaged in a career, a meaningful relationship, or an important endeavor, you need get out of your goldfish bowl.

Think about the implications of that.

If you want to be an entrepreneur or a doctor, an architect or a carpenter, an artist or a politician, a great mom or dad or partner—whatever you want to be—your normal first step would be to get the appropriate education or training, apprentice yourself to a successful mentor, or just dive in and learn as you go. But all of these approaches start with your existing mind, which is subject to all the problems I've mentioned. Wouldn't it be better to upgrade your thinking first? Otherwise all your learning and experience will be built inside your goldfish bowl.

As well or as poorly as you and I have navigated our lives up to this point, couldn't we do better? I know I could, and I know I want to. I assume you want the same or are at least open to the possibility.

That's the purpose of this book: to help us escape our goldfish bowls by retraining our unconscious minds so they serve us better and help us avoid going stupid. If we can do that, we have unlimited possibilities.

Your mantra should be "First my mind, then my life."

So hang in there with me, and together we'll upgrade our thinking a little bit or a lot and, in doing so, upgrade our lives a little bit or a lot.

CHAPTER ONE

How I Learned All This Stuff, and Why I Know It Works

You may be asking yourself, who is this guy Alexander, and why does he think he has answers that others don't? Why should I take this book seriously?

To answer those questions, I'll start with a little bit of history. I'll show you where these ideas came from and how they're working for thousands and thousands of small business owners, managers, and students who have been coached with methods similar to those described in this book.

For me, it all began in 1995 when I joined Michael Gerber and his team of small business coaches, then calling themselves the Gerber Business Development Company. Everybody should have a Michael Gerber in his life. Michael is irascible, demanding, impatient, and simply cannot pass up an opportunity; he's the consummate entrepreneur. He's also brilliant, deeply compassionate, and loving, not to mention impish and more than a little profane. To this day, I both love and hate him, and he knows it. I suspect he wouldn't have it any other way.

If you want to get a sense of Michael's thinking and the principles that underlie good business development, you've got to read his book *The E-Myth Revisited* (E-Myth stands for Entrepreneurial Myth). It's a must-read for business people and would-be entrepreneurs, and, according to the Wall Street Journal, it's the all-time best-selling book on small business management.

Business coaching is the practice of teaching others how to create and manage businesses and mentoring them through the process. That's what we were doing in those days, but at a deeper level, we were doing something else as well, something more important and fundamental. We were helping our clients shift their conscious and unconscious habits of mind.

While we were teaching business principles and helping our clients apply them to their businesses, we were also helping them overcome their unconscious thinking, shifting their beliefs, replacing dysfunctional habits of mind with new ones, and tapping into their most deeply held senses of purpose and motivation. In other words, using business as the focus of attention, we enabled them to convert their flawed thinking and illusions of mind into the beginnings of true entrepreneurship. And it was no small thing that as we helped our clients improve their businesses, they reported to us that their lives outside of their businesses also improved.

Michael Gerber was the pioneer for this kind of business coaching, beginning in the 1970s and continuing to this day. I joined him in the mid-1990s and was the catalyst for creating his leading-edge, never-been-done-before E-Myth Mastery Program. It was my job to create the written materials and practices that hundreds of coaches used daily to teach and mentor thousands and thousands of clients in all industries and in a dozen nations around the world. I converted the practical, hard-won knowledge gained by Michael and his team over the decades into a disciplined program that was teachable by any coach and useable by any client.

And it worked. Beautifully. At the time, it was the most advanced coaching method available anywhere. Michael's organization, rebranded as the E-Myth Academy, became the preeminent small business coaching organization in the world.

I left Michael Gerber's organization in the year 2000 after wrapping up the E-Myth Mastery program for him. My work there was complete, so I moved into academia, where I taught business management and leadership at Menlo College and Santa Clara University, both in California's Silicon Valley. Business principles are business principles no matter where you learn them, so much of my teaching was pretty straightforward, similar to teaching engineering. But leadership teaching was something very different, very personal. My favorite was a course called Leadership, Creativity, and Ethics, which relied on many of the principles and practices you'll see in this book. I taught college kids and, in the adult education program, working adults of all ages and in a wide variety of occupations, all of them wanting to create the best possible careers (and lives) for themselves.

The results were bimodal—either spectacularly successful or a complete bust. The people who engaged in the process, the ones who were willing to learn new habits of mind and open themselves up to new possibilities, did well. The students who regarded the work as tasks to be completed for a grade or to please a teacher made little or no progress. The same had been true in business coaching—the unengaged people were the people who dropped out of the coaching program after a few months, making no progress and believing the program had failed them. In reality, they had failed themselves by giving in to their old habits of mind, always looking for the easy shortcut and, in doing so, perpetuating business-as-usual and, more disappointingly, life-as-usual.

The business owners and managers who engaged in the process put themselves on the path to leadership and entrepreneurship and made strides in their personal lives as they did so. The successful students gave me feedback testifying to better grades and a more successful classroom experience. The adult education students reported more success in their jobs as well as feedback from coworkers and bosses that showed that their business skills and their leadership potential had improved, often remarkably so.

Two examples:

John was a worker in a local municipal government. After about three weeks in my Leadership, Creativity, and Ethics course, John told me that his coworkers were telling him they had noticed improvements in his attitude, helpfulness, and general approach to his work. After about five weeks, he reported that his boss was saying the same thing. By the end of the twelve-week course, John reported that he had been promoted to a managerial position. John credited the course for his success.

Jane, a personal organization consultant, reported conflicts with her most important client and that she was expecting the client to fire her soon. At about the fifth week of the course, Jane reported that her client had noticed a sharp improvement in Jane's services and attitude and not only increased her usage of Jane's services but also referred Jane to her friends.

In 2005, I left academia and formed a team of experienced business coaches in the USA and Australia, raised the necessary startup money, and launched a new company, doing business as the Full Spectrum Coaching Company. Our objective was and still is to help small business owners worldwide improve their businesses and, in doing so, improve their lives. My first task was to create an entirely new, leading-edge coaching program. It took four years of development, experimentation, and writing, but we pulled it off. The result is the Full Spectrum Business Development Program, and by all reports from users, it's superior to anything else in the field of business coaching, including the E-Myth Mastery Program that I developed for Michael Gerber years earlier.

Concurrently with my academic work, I self-educated by devouring the available literature on the workings of the mind. While I don't have a doctoral degree in psychology, my studies of mind science dovetailed beautifully with my coaching and teaching work, focused as it was on changing the ways that business owners, entrepreneurs, and students think and behave.

Because I was coaching and educating real people, I had access to a real-world laboratory. Probably even better than the scientists themselves, I had the means to create theories, test them, and use the results to synthesize methods for helping people upgrade their thinking. The result: improved mind power for anyone who's interested and motivated.

So that's the history.

But does this stuff work? And how does it work? How does it help you escape your counterproductive habits of mind—your goldfish bowl—and convert your unconscious biases and questionable beliefs into clarity of mind and good decision-making? How does it help you escape the illusion of clarity and help you achieve the real thing? Bottom line question: Does it enable people to upgrade their mind power?

Here's how the process is working in the real world for our business clients and students.

Clients typically come to us in a state of confusion and frustration. Their businesses aren't working, and they don't know why. Because they've tried everything they know and none of it has worked for them, they come to us receptive to new possibilities—often reluctant, but open to new thinking and to looking at themselves in new ways. That's critically important. If they're not open to new thinking, and merely expect us to fix them and their businesses, they won't truly engage in the process.

Engaged in the process means that they're willing to try some new ways of thinking and act on those new thoughts. In order to do that, they have to become more open to possibilities than they've been in the past, they have to look more critically at the realities of their businesses and themselves, and they have to think creatively.

We start by asking our clients to take a look inside themselves. We like to say, "First your mind, then your business." This step starts the process of breaking old habits of mind. We help them discover their deeply held inner motivation, which we call Core Purpose. They sometimes do this skeptically, not initially seeing the value in it but giving it a try anyway. Those who engage in the process come away with something precious, a bedrock source of purpose and motivation in their lives. The unengaged ones go through the motions, but in actuality, they never really get it.

Next, we ask our clients to take their minds out of their daily grind and think strategically about general business principles. It's the beginning of strategic thinking, and it's a fundamental aspect of the entrepreneurial mind. We start them off by suggesting some new beliefs and ways of thinking that open them up to more possibilities than they were accustomed to imagining.

Then we get specific and focus on the client's own business, seeing how fundamental business principles and new ways of thinking apply in their unique situations. We do this through a series of practices with names like Strategic Intent (thinking about what they want the business to look like when it's mature and successful), Strategic Action (making the right strategic decisions about the business), Business Organization (identifying the work the business must accomplish, and what activities (jobs) are necessary to get that work done), and more. What's happening is that by doing the work of developing their businesses, they're developing new habits of thinking. They don't set out to create new ways of thinking, but that's what they're unconsciously doing as they work on their businesses through practice, repetition, and the willingness to try new ideas.

The longer they stay in the program—experimenting with new beliefs about business and about themselves, practicing new habits of mind by doing the work of building their businesses, and shedding huge chunks of their unproductive thinking in favor of a new entrepreneurial mindset—the more they develop.

Yes, of course their businesses get better—much better—and so do their lives.

The practices I'm offering you work, but only if you engage them. If you merely go through the motions, you'll waste your time and make little or no progress, and you'll blame me for offering something that you think doesn't work. If you don't engage, your old habits of mind will continue to dominate, and you'll get the same results that you've always gotten in your career and your life. That's okay with me if it's okay with you, but it's regrettable because so much more is possible.

CHAPTER TWO

A Layman's Tour of Mind Science

Simplifying the Science So We Can Use It

I'm not going to repeat the science. It's too academic, technical, and dense. But you need to know some basics, so I'm going to simplify and summarize it for you.

There's a potential problem with simplifying something as complex as the human mind. As you'll see later in this book, simplification is one of the mind traps that we need to avoid because simplification can distort the reality out of a situation and bias our understanding. To complicate matters, our minds are built to think that simplification is smart when often it's not.

On the other hand, simplifying the complex, if done thoughtfully, can be useful, even necessary. Think of the automobile as an analogy. The science of an automobile includes a lot of metallurgy, electrical engineering, chemistry, physics, and other sciences, but in order to make use of an automobile, we don't need to know any of that. All we need to know is how to operate and care for our cars.

This book does that for our minds. It honors and obeys the science without subjecting us to its complexity and does so in a way that preserves scientific integrity. It presents the science in a more understandable, more useful form using simpler, common sense terminology. It tells us how better to operate and care for our conscious and unconscious minds without becoming scientists.

If you want to learn more about mind science—and I highly recommend that you do—I have listed my favorite ten books about mind science. You'll find that list in Attachment A. It's a good place to start.

That said, let's take a simplified look at the science of the mind.

Brain or Mind?

The brain exists in a black box—the skull—which has access to the outside world and the body only through the senses. Incoming sensory information stimulates the brain, which responds with complex bioelectrochemical processes.

The brain is a highly complex system—the most complex system we know about. Complex systems can produce what are called "emergent properties," which arise from the system but in ways science can't always explain. We identify these emergent properties with names like consciousness, thoughts, ideas, emotions, intuitions, awareness, and many habits of thinking, including cognitive biases. All of these emergent phenomena are collectively known as "the mind."

David Eagleman, prominent neuroscientist and author of the book *Incognito: The Secret Lives of the Brain*, has this to say when he describes the idea of emergence and the relationship between brain and mind:

> When you put together large numbers of pieces and parts [complexity], the whole can become something greater than the sum. None of the individual metal hunks of an airplane have the property of flight, but when they are attached together in the right way, the result takes to the air. A thin metal bar won't do you much good if you're trying to control a jaguar, but several of them in parallel have the property of containment. The concept of emergent properties means that something new can be introduced that is not inherent in any of the parts.

The brain is matter; the mind is not. We know the mind exists because we experience it. We know it emerges from brain activity because we can make specific bioelectrochemical changes to the brain and experience predictable and specific changes in the mind.

The brain is malleable; it physically changes and adapts as a result of our learning and experience. It does this with no intention on our part, and it does so automatically throughout our lives. Changing the way the nonmaterial mind behaves—the way we think—actually changes the physical structure and operation of the material brain.

Mind Behavior

We are conscious beings, meaning that we are aware of ourselves and our environment, and we can voluntarily shift our awareness and attention as needed. We can directly control those aspects of our thoughts that are within our awareness—within our conscious thinking. We also have extensive thinking that is not within our awareness and is not directly controlled by our conscious thinking, although, as we will see later in this book, it can be indirectly controlled. Unconscious thinking makes up the vast majority of our mental activity.

Our sensory abilities bring information into our conscious awareness and even more information into our *unconscious* minds. Our minds process these sensory inputs based on thoughts, felt senses, attitudes, beliefs, emotions, and even some of our personality traits. Felt senses, if you're not familiar with the term, include such sensations as gut feel, tension, tingling, the exhilaration that accompanies an "aha" moment, and many other reactions we feel in our bodies but which originate in our brains. All of this mental activity results in understandings—mental models—of ourselves and the external world.

We also have memories, which are recollections of past things and events that include thoughts themselves. Memories are not exact recordings of data but mental reconstructions of past events and things. Our memories and mental models add up to our *perceptions* of ourselves and the world around us, and they're not always accurate for reasons that we'll explore later.

Associations, Interconnectedness, Interdependency, and Enormous Complexity...All of It Beneath the Surface

We all know the metaphor of a duck swimming on a pond; the duck appears calm and placid above the water while its feet are churning wildly beneath the surface. That's like your mind. Above the surface in your conscious mind, things seem relatively straightforward while below the surface in your unconscious mind, an enormous number of connections and impulses are wildly churning here and there at incredible speeds and with even more incredible complexity. You're not aware of them, although you're completely dependent upon them for your very survival and sanity.

I bring up the subject of complexity and interconnectedness for a reason, and this is something you need to grasp because it is one of the keys for learning how to guide and direct your own unconscious thinking. One of the most miraculous things your brain does with all of its complexity is create unconscious associations.

Every moment you live your life and think your thoughts, your brain is creating associations, and these associations are assembled from all of your sensory perceptions, your conscious and unconscious thoughts, memories, emotions—anything that is detected or generated by your conscious and unconscious mind.

Think of an experience you've had, say your first moments of middle school back when you were about thirteen years old. The experience included a bewildering array of sensory input: the noise of hundreds of other kids; new sights of buildings, school grounds, rooms, hallways, styles of clothing, and a lot more. There were probably odors such as perfume on some of the girls, food cooking in the school cafeteria, and things in the classrooms, like chalk or fresh paint. The noise was probably deafening with hundreds of kids excitedly talking, school bells counting down the start of the first class, and the school public address system yelling over it all. Tactile sensations were there too, such as the feel of the railing on the stairwell, the touch of the combination lock on your school locker (if you had one), or the texture of the desktop when you settled in for your first class. You couldn't help but feel all kinds of emotions. Depending on your personality, you might have been overwhelmed by excitement, anxiety, or curiosity but certainly not boredom or indifference. As you read this paragraph, you're undoubtedly thinking of dozens of things I've neglected to mention, all of them associations your own mind established based on your own unique experience.

From that day on, when you smell chalk, walk down a stairwell that has a rail with a similar texture to the one in your middle school, smell cafeteria food, or encounter any of hundreds (even thousands) of other impressions associated in your mind with that day, much of the day will come alive in your mind. The more intense the emotions of the day, the more lasting and intense the associations will be. Ask any veteran of the Vietnam War what happens when she/he hears a helicopter. Ask any heart attack survivor what happens when she/he smells a certain kind of plastic, the kind that oxygen hoses are made of. Ask anyone what happens when you say the word "mother."

Anything that ever happened to you had a context. There were sounds, sights, smells, textures, tastes, thoughts, emotions, and intuitions happening as well as other multilayered associations connected with them. The more intense the experience, the more deeply imbedded the associations. Intensity has a lot to do with emotion.

It's through discovering existing associations and creating new ones that we can bring conscious intention rather than automatic reaction to our unconscious minds and much of our conscious decision-making.

Your Unconscious Mind Is In Charge

The unconscious mind is something we don't pay much attention to because it's invisible to us. It operates automatically and with blinding speed. It learns when we don't know it's learning, and sometimes it learns things that are false. We don't control it, although we can learn to. By far, it's the source of most of our mental processes. And, by way of flawed habits of mind, it's the main reason we sometimes go stupid.

Bad news: your unconscious mind dominates your thinking.

Dominates? Really?

Yes, really.

Did you know that when you make a conscious decision, your unconscious mind has already processed that decision? Decisions are made by the unconscious mind and then either allowed or negated by the conscious mind. Mind/brain scientists have measured both the sequence—first unconscious, then conscious—and the elapsed time, which is about three-tenths of a second between the instant your unconscious mind processes the decision and the instant your conscious mind registers it. Even when we feel that our conscious minds are directing our thoughts and actions, in actuality, we're mainly driven by our unconscious minds.

The *unconscious* mind is the leader. The conscious mind is the follower. It doesn't *feel* like that, but that's the way it is. Neuroscience consistently proves and re-proves it.

Fortunately, your conscious mind has the ability take charge and put itself in the leadership position. It does so either by negating unconscious decisions or by deliberately and consciously creating unconscious habits of mind involved in decision-making. Yes, you can reshape your unconscious thinking. That's critical because the *conscious* mind is the driver of intentionality and purpose, and only when the conscious mind is in the leadership position can intentional, rather than habitual, thinking emerge.

Let's examine unconscious thinking a bit more closely, and you'll see what I mean.

Did you know that at least 95 percent of your thinking and perceiving happens *un*consciously? It's true, and it's a good thing because if you had to think and do everything consciously, you'd go nuts.

Some things, actually *most* things, are best left to our unconscious mental processes, especially routine, repetitive activities like walking, reading, chewing, and thousands of other activities. On the other hand, some things need to be dealt with consciously because they're new, risky, or important, and because the unconscious mind sometimes encounters contradictions and paradoxes, and the conscious mind has to step in to resolve them.

First, if you've never thought about it, take a moment to convince yourself that most of your mental processes are unconscious.

Take the simple act of reading—what you're doing right now. When you first started reading as a toddler, you laboriously (and consciously) learned the alphabet. After a while, you could recite your ABCs automatically and unconsciously. Then you consciously learned the sounds of the letters. After a while, the sounds were automatically associated with the letters, and you didn't have to think consciously about them any more. Then you learned about spelling: C-A-T. Then came sentences, paragraphs, and ultimately whole books.

Now when you read, do you think about the letters? The sounds? Are you aware of sentence structure? Do you have to translate words into ideas? No. You do it all automatically and unconsciously. What you do consciously is think about the ideas and images that your unconscious mind extracted from the letters, words, punctuation, paragraphs, and pages. When you read a book, a newspaper, or a product label, your unconscious mind does all the hard work so your conscious mind will be free to deal with the ideas your unconscious mind extracted from ink spots on a page or pixels on a screen.

What happens when you encounter an unfamiliar word or bad grammar in your reading? Even if it's just for a moment, it pops you out of unconscious thinking into conscious thinking, doesn't it? Then you decide what to do about it. You can look up the unfamiliar word, figure out its meaning from the context, or simply ignore it. The same kind of thing happens when you're driving your car. You're buzzing along, listening to the radio or talking with a friend while your driving is taken care of automatically by your unconscious mind. But when something unexpected occurs, say another driver swerves in front of you, you pop out of unconscious thinking, and your conscious mind instantly gets involved to cope with the situation. When the situation becomes routine again, your conscious mind moves on to other things, and you ease back into unconscious driving.

A lot of your unconscious thinking was learned *un*consciously. For instance, most of us can tell when someone is sad. How did you learn to detect that people are sad, happy, stressed, or angry? You learned from experience by seeing human behavior and unconsciously picking up little clues here and there. The older you got, the better you became at detecting people's moods. It works like that for any of the thousands of other things that you don't consciously think about, the things you just know.

By the way, don't make the mistake of believing that your thinking is either conscious or unconscious. Your brain doesn't have a toggle switch that's in either the conscious or the unconscious position. Your conscious and unconscious thinking are always interdependent. Your unconscious thinking is always feeding impressions to your conscious mind, and your conscious mind is always deciding what to do about them and feeding that thinking back into your unconscious mind in millions of endless loops. Even such conscious activities as conversing with friends depends upon the unconscious mind's ability to detect and decipher sounds and deliver their meaning to your conscious mind. You consciously deal with the ideas while your unconscious mind is receiving sound signals, comparing them with your mental models, adding whatever emotional component it finds appropriate, and feeding its conclusions to your conscious mind.

When things are routine, nonthreatening, and generally meet with your expectations, your unconscious thinking dominates your actions. But when you're surprised, threatened, or conflicted, your conscious thinking gets involved until the situation is resolved. Your unconscious mind is still engaged—it never stops—and most of your mental activity continues to be of the unconscious sort. Your conscious thinking is still taking in all the impressions provided by your unconscious thinking, reacting to your beliefs and mental models about the way the world works. In general, conscious thinking still depends on the unconscious mind for a sense of right and wrong, expectations about what will happen next, and for the emotional responses that give meaning to it all.

In other words, even though your conscious thinking is fully engaged, that conscious thinking continues to be concurrently shaped by your unconscious mind, just as your unconscious mind concurrently adjusts to what your conscious mind is doing. It's more than a feedback loop; it's a completely integrated, interdependent process.

Innate Biases

Beware! Your unconscious mind can and sometimes does deceive you. Let me pass on a few simplified and paraphrased examples of what the experts in the field of brains and minds tell us about our unconscious thinking and some of the ways it is innately biased.

> If we like something, or if it stimulates pleasant emotions, our unconscious minds are more likely to perceive it as factual, accurate, correct, and right, whether or not it actually is. If we're aware of this effect, our conscious minds can override such false impressions, but most of us don't know about it. So, when our unconscious minds make us "feel" like something is right, even when it's not, we usually accept it as right.

> If we're familiar with an idea, our unconscious minds also perceive it as correct and good, again, whether or not it actually is. The same is true of repetition of ideas. The more they are repeated, and if we have no preconceived opinions about them, the more we perceive them as correct and right. Advertisers and propa-

gandists all know this. Again, if we know about it, our conscious minds can overcome this dysfunctional effect.

If an idea is easy to grasp—simple, clear, brief—our unconscious minds tend to perceive it as correct and right, whether or not it is, compared with a more complex, harder to understand idea. That's why people so often take the simpler idea as true, and ignore or pooh-pooh the reality of a more complex idea. By the way, Occam's Razor—the principle that the simplest of two or more competing theories is preferable—is false. Neither simplicity nor complexity makes something true. Reality is what it is, whether simple or complex.

If people we like and/or trust tell us something, our unconscious minds perceive it as correct and right, unless we have other preconceptions, and even then we might override our preconceptions if our faith in the person telling us is strong enough.

Our conscious and unconscious minds tend to give more credibility and greater importance to recently learned information, as compared with information learned further in the past.

This is just a sampling of what has been discovered about the workings of our unconscious minds. There's a lot more, and more is being discovered every day.

In summary, a huge amount of our thinking is done unconsciously, and most of our conscious thinking is shaped by our unconscious minds; however, if we're aware enough, the conscious mind has the ability to modify our unconscious thinking.

There Are Two Truths for Everything: Reality A and Reality B

For every situation, there is an actual, factual reality; something exists, or something happened. That's what I call Reality A, and it's the objective, actual reality (the factual reality) of the world outside of our minds.

Separately from Reality A, there is our internal experience of that reality. That's what I call Reality B, which is our subjective, inner perception. They're not always the same. In fact, they're never the same because one is external and real in the world outside of our skulls, and the other is our perception of it, an idea within our minds or what some have called an internal representation of reality.

Reality A is simply what exists. It is what it is.

Reality B is what we perceive it to be.

A lot of the struggle of life is the attempt to create an internal understanding—Reality B—in our minds that matches up with the facts of Reality A. Many problems in life happen when we get it wrong, when Reality B doesn't match up with Reality A.

Reality B is a lot like a road map. It's a representation of something in the world, but it's not the thing itself. A map of the road from home to work is not the same as the actual road from home to work, but if the map faithfully represents that road, then it's a very useful thing. If the map is in error, it's worse than useless. It misleads us. It lies to us. And any decisions or actions we take based on an erroneous map will lead us astray.

Within our minds, our internal Reality B seems to be the one and only actual reality. We don't know when it's in error unless we know how to engage our conscious minds and force ourselves to become aware that our internal reality is different from the external reality.

Why does Reality B stray from the factuality of Reality A? It's because our minds process and interpret the factual data that our senses detect. We process and reshape it based on our beliefs, expectations, and the way our minds work.

For example, the eyes and ears report facts: a loud noise, a flash of light, and the direction they come from. Based on experience, what has been learned in the past and some beliefs, the mind interprets these factual observations and concludes, "thunder and lightning." But that's not all that's attached to the experience. Centuries ago, part of the experience was fear because it was believed that thunder was an expression of the anger of the gods, and the ancient observer might have prayed or made a sacrifice to appease those gods.

Reality A was thunder and lightning. Reality B was angry gods.

Fast forward to today. Because of education and prevailing beliefs, the modern observer still perceives thunder and lightning, but the experience also includes thoughts about clouds, wind, and, depending on the individual's education, associated ideas about static electricity and electric currents heating up the air so quickly that a sonic boom is created. If there is fear, it's not fear of the gods' anger but anxiety about getting wet or, if close enough, fear of a lightning strike.

Thunder and lightning are what they are; they're factual, but the minds of observers can generate radically different inner perceptions of them. Because of our internal processing, Reality A (the factual reality) can give rise to a different and distorted Reality B (the experiential reality).

Here's a more contemporary example:

We're in a courtroom. Two eyewitnesses—young women in their early twenties, friends, who were walking together—saw two men fighting. They observed the fight from the same place at the same time. They witnessed one and only one event, one and only one Reality A. But look at the differences in their Reality Bs. Witness #1 says, "I saw the defendant attack the plaintiff for no reason." Witness

#2, thinking the defendant was reacting to a perceived threat, says, "I saw the defendant take a swing at the plaintiff, but he was simply protecting himself."

Again, a single Reality A gives rise to different and contradictory Reality Bs. There was only one actual event, but the minds of the two witnesses contain contradictory perceptions.

My point, and forgive me for being Captain Obvious, is that we all create mental models of reality. We have to; we're built that way. Usually our mental models serve us well, but often, for all kinds of reasons, our models can be flawed, even though we completely and sincerely, consciously and unconsciously, believe them to be *the* reality.

Here's the problem: We base our actions on the internal experience of Reality B, not the factuality of Reality A, because Reality B is all our minds know. Our minds—trapped within our goldfish bowls—fully believe that B *is* A. When our internal realities are flawed, which they sometimes are, we make mistakes, and our actions fall short of our expectations or fail completely—we go stupid. The more complex the reality, the less we understand it, and the more flawed our Reality B is likely to be. The consequences can be trivial. For example, does it really matter if some people still think thunder is an expression of angry gods? On the other hand, they can be enormously consequential. Adolf Hitler's Reality B killed millions, and Martin Luther King Jr.'s Reality B made millions of lives better.

Reality B matters—a lot. When our Reality B reflects the factuality of the world, it creates the opportunity for greater success, happiness, and leadership that results in widespread well-being. When it doesn't track with factuality, it can lead to mistakes (sometimes catastrophic mistakes) and widespread misery.

Because of this, it's critical—*critical!*—either that your Reality B is a fair representation of Reality A or that when it's not, you can admit to not knowing rather than insisting on a flawed Reality B. Often, if not always, "I don't know" is a far better position to take than the certainty of a false Reality B.

So the all-important question is "How can I know when my Reality B is flawed or incomplete?" Even more importantly, you should ask, "How can I make sure that my Reality B is as close to the real-world Reality A as possible?" We'll get to that.

Original Mind and Conditioning

What Is Original Mind?

The story of your mind started in the womb, when all those millions of neural cells and connections began to shape themselves into the beginnings of your brain. But the real story began at birth when you became able to interact with the outside world, not just sense its vibrations but actually perceive and interact with it.

At the moment of your birth, you were a bundle of instinctual behavior with a nascent temperament but no conscious thinking, completely dependent on the outside world for everything, and aware (if it could be called awareness) only that you felt good or bad. You didn't have words for good or bad, but you felt them. Your bodily functions and movements were random, purposeless, and automatic. You had no knowledge, opinions, values, habits, or experiences. You couldn't form a conscious thought of any kind. Words were just random noise. The world was a swirling vortex of meaningless sensory input. What you saw, heard, smelled, felt, and tasted…all meaningless.

It would have been confusing if you had the ability to be confused, but even that had not yet developed. You couldn't do anything but eat, eliminate, and, when you didn't feel good, cry.

You weren't even you yet. You had a few tendencies, the early stirrings of what would become your personality, but nothing resembling a real personality or identity. Undoubtedly, you already had your soul, but I'm not really sure what a soul is, and I'm not foolish enough to tackle the subject of the soul in this book. The mind is challenge enough.

So there you were—alive and in possession of a miraculous body (partially developed) and the beginnings of a mind that would be shaped by others in your early years.

Yet with all your helplessness, dependency, and lack of conscious thought, this original mind of yours was the most open, objective, and creative it would ever be.

From this point on, I'm going to capitalize Original Mind to emphasize its importance. It's the foundation of everything you have become. As you'll see, your Original Mind got distorted and suppressed as you grew and matured. It wasn't your fault. It was the normal functioning of your mind and your natural responses to the conditioning imposed on you by your own needs and the environment around you. And it wasn't a bad thing. In fact, it was a very good thing. You couldn't function, then or now, without all that early conditioning.

Original Mind has three main characteristics: openness, objectivity, and creativity. Let me tell you about them and how your early conditioning gradually diminished them and maybe even shut them down.

Openness

Openness is the ability to consider all ideas and beliefs and allow for all possibilities, even those that don't agree with your beliefs and perceptions. It's the ability to see and understand any and all points of view, even those you know to be false. You may not agree with them, but you're willing to understand them and also understand how and why others believe them, however false they may seem to you.

At birth and during your early infancy, you were open to anything and everything. Whatever reached your senses simply poured into you. You let everything in. No filters. No blocks. No distortions. No preconceived ideas about what you were sensing. You weren't interested in some things and disinterested in others—not at first. You were a sponge, absorbing anything and everything your senses detected.

What Happened?

Very quickly you were conditioned to pay attention to and pre-fer some things and not others. You developed expectations, experiences, and interpretations that colored the way your mind perceived what your senses were letting in. You created conscious and unconscious models of the way the world is, but your ability to see things that didn't fit these models diminished, and what you saw was adjusted by your mind, consciously and uncon-sciously, to conform with what you thought you knew to be true. You still *feel* open and receptive—everybody does—but your mind, consciously and unconsciously, ignores much of what it's exposed to and adjusts what you perceive to be consistent with your conditioning—your perception of what's true and what's false. And you're unaware that it's happening.

Objectivity

Objectivity is a universal human trait at birth but one of the rarest of human traits after a few years of life. It's the ability to perceive reality as it actually is.

Objectivity is not the lack of bias or preference. It's the ability to see through—to ignore—bias or preference. It's the ability to withhold judgment until you have enough information to make an informed judgment.

At birth and for a short time afterward, you saw things as they actually were. You perceived reality rather than a distorted version of reality. You didn't understand what you were seeing, but whatever it was, you saw it clearly, cleanly, and with no distortions. You had no judgments about anything. Well, food and cuddling felt good, so you probably had some rudimentary, unconscious judgments, but other than that, everything was what it was, with no overlay of judgment, expectation, correct or incorrect, right or wrong, good or bad.

What Happened?

You slowly began to see things as good or bad, likeable or unlikeable, mean or kind. Your perceptions were first shaped by how they impacted you (pleasure or discomfort), later by what Mom and Dad told you, and still later depending on what was normal and acceptable in the community you were a part of. You were told what's true and what's false, what's real and what's unreal. You learned should and should not, and your set of values and ethics began to take shape. People like you and those within your community became "we" and others became "they." "We" were seen as good, correct, desirable, supportive, and normal while "they" became bad, mistaken (or lying), abhorrent, antagonistic, and abnormal. Your sense of identity took on a strong self-centered bias, so that your assessment of your own abilities and achievements exaggerated the positive and minimized the negative or sometimes vice versa, and self-deception began to raise its ugly head.

Your objectivity was slowly but inexorably conditioned out of you by the natural functioning of your mind, an ego that wants to be superior, and a family and community that immersed you in its ways of thinking and believing.

All this happened long before you had the ability to make judgments and think for yourself. By the time you had developed the potential for making your own judgments and shaping your own thinking, most of the unconscious habits of mind that make you what you are today had already been conditioned into you so deeply that they seemed to be your innate self. They still do.

Creativity

At birth, your creative mechanism was already in place. Creativity is all about unconscious connectivity (associations) and holistic processing in the brain. In essence, creativity works like this: your unconscious mind feeds upon everything available to it—information, memories, thoughts, experiences, and bodily sensations—and it makes connections, sees patterns (which may or may not really exist), and seeks to form coherent impressions, and then it delivers the results to the conscious mind in the form of impressions, conclusions, ideas, and aha moments. When you were born, you didn't have knowledge or experience, which are the fuel that powers creativity, but, because of its ability to make associations, the creative mechanism in your brain was in place from the beginning. Because the conscious mind isn't privy to all this unconscious processing, creativity seems mysterious, almost magical. But it's not. It's simply the normal workings of the unconscious mind.

What Happened?

You were taught what's possible and impossible, what's acceptable and unacceptable, what's right and wrong, what's real and imaginary, what's good and bad, and what's inevitable and what's controllable. What you learned may or may not actually be so, but it's what you learned, and it became what you *believe*—your perception of reality. Belief operates both consciously and unconsciously, and what's in your mind is all that your creativity has to work with, so in the unconscious mind, opinions and assumptions, however ill-founded, are taken as reality, and the unconscious mind builds coherent understandings based on these so-called realities. The result is unconscious thinking that's often questionable and creativity that's channeled, limited, and sometimes blocked by what it has to work with and what it lacks.

Original Mind—openness, objectivity, and creativity—is still a part of each of us, but it has been buried and distorted under our lifetimes of conditioning. Our conditioning is the water we swim in, and it's the goldfish bowl holding the water. It's insidious conditioning because we're not aware of it. How could we be? In the early years, we couldn't even form a conscious thought, and by the time we could, we were already conditioned into habits of mind and beliefs not of our own choosing.

It may be life's greatest irony that all of this suppression and distortion has been done and is being done with love and the best of intentions by people and institutions who think they're doing right by us. It's another grand irony that, in order to break out of our fish bowls, we need to regain the state of Original Mind. No, we can't, and no, we don't want to return to the ignorance and dependency of infancy, but we do need to regain an adult version of Original Mind: openness, objectivity, and creativity. We'll see how to do that in later chapters.

Habits of Mind

We have many habitual thought processes, and they shift and change as we learn, mature, and experience our lives. When stimulated (triggered), they operate automatically based on prior conditioning. Our conditioning is the result of learning and experience, modified by feedback loops that enable us to adjust. Habits of mind can be conscious, unconscious, or a combination. There are two kinds of mental habits:

- *Cognitive habits* (habits of thinking)

    Cognitive habits are routine and automatic ways of thinking that have been learned or conditioned into us. They operate somewhat like subroutines in a computer program.

    A special and very important subset of cognitive habits is that of *cognitive biases*, which I mentioned earlier. Cognitive biases are those habits of thinking which, in some situations, can lead us astray, cause us to make mistakes, form erroneous mental models, generate false beliefs, and make us behave in ineffective and sometimes harmful ways.

There are hundreds of cognitive biases that have been identified and studied by the psychological/psychiatric community, and it's a growing list. Seven years ago, Wikipedia listed 126 cognitive biases. As of this writing, the list has increased to 220. This book focuses our attention on what I consider to be the most problematic cognitive biases and shows how we can correct them.

- *Personality habits* (habits of being or traits)

  Personality habits are the answers to the question "What kind of person am I?" We describe personality habits with words such as courageous, timid, aggressive, curious, conscientious, hardworking, conflict avoiding, generous, and scores more, if not hundreds.

In some circumstances, certain personality habits can interfere with our thinking and behavior. For instance, if we tend to have aggressive personalities, our aggressiveness can be strengths in some situations but weaknesses—dysfunctional habits—at other times. We can identify and change personality habits just as we can identify and change cognitive habits, although, as you'll see, dealing with dysfunctional personality habits can be more challenging than dealing with cognitive biases.

The latest theories indicate that we are born with some innate tendencies, and we are also born with a basic set of temperamental traits, which form our rudimentary personalities. As we grow and mature, our tendencies and our rudimentary personalities mature into their adult forms, but the underlying patterns remain. We have the ability to overcome or modify our habits of mind, and we can do so at any age, so when our habits of mind aren't serving us as well as they should, we have the ability to change them.

A Model of the Mind

Let's put this overview of mind science into a model that will help us upgrade our minds. Any model is an artificial construct, a simplification—sort of like the map I mentioned earlier, which is a representation of a physical reality but is not that reality. Our model of the mind is designed to help us understand and correct the mental processes that cause most of our mistakes and misunderstandings. It shows us where to place our attention in order to recondition our minds so that going stupid becomes far less likely.

The diagram below illustrates the model, and the following discussion talks about the elements of the diagram. The model illustrates the two aspects of reality—the actual reality and the perception of it—as well as the obstacle course our minds create when we process our sensory data through our mental filters.

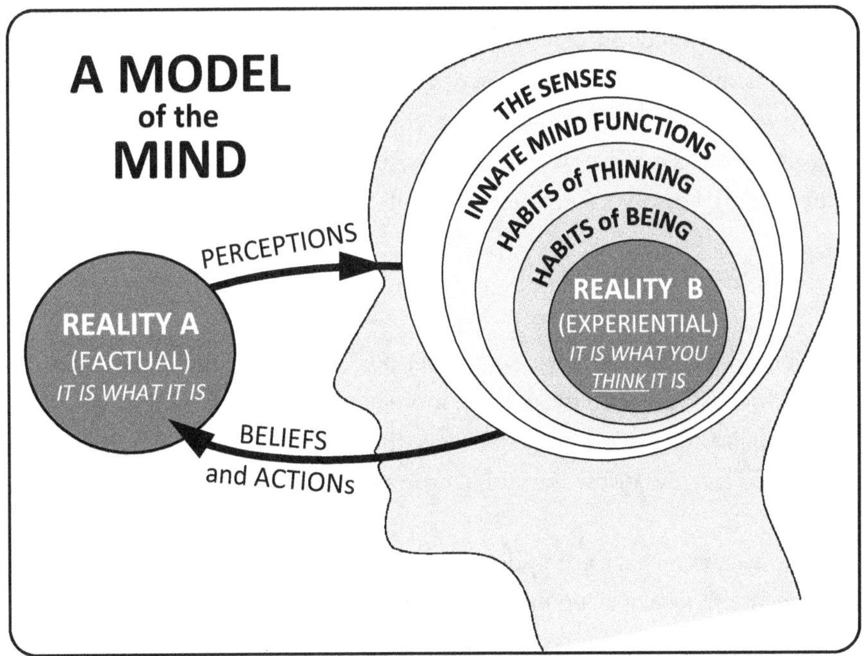

Reality A and Reality B

Reality A is the actual object or event that occurs in the real world outside of our minds. Reality B is what we perceive it to be after we take in our sensory information and our minds process it through our innate mind functions, habits of thinking, and habits of being.

When Reality B aligns with Reality A, our perceptions are accurate, and the conclusions we draw and judgments we make are likely to be accurate and sound. When Reality B is not aligned with Reality A, we jump to false conclusions, make avoidable mistakes, and take inappropriate actions.

The Senses

The senses receive information from the outside world: sight, sound, taste, smell, and touch, plus a few other senses like balance, temperature, and sense of direction. Even before our minds process these sensory inputs, we can get them wrong. Optical illusions, interferences (i.e., conflicting bright lights, confusing noises, complex aromas, weather effects), the way we focus or fail to focus our attention, and many other distractions can interfere with the accuracy of our senses, and all that can happen before sensory information even gets into the mind.

Innate Mind Functions

I mentioned innate biases earlier. Remember, our unconscious minds prefer simplicity, repetition of ideas can make them more believable to us, we tend to believe what's familiar and are less likely to believe the unfamiliar, and so on. Our unconscious mind can also distort our thinking in other ways.

Our unconscious minds can only deal with the information that's available to them, and they aren't aware when information is missing, incomplete, or inaccurate. Thus we can draw conclusions, create impressions, and develop intuitions that are consistent with flawed information, leading to mistakes which, even though they're mistakes, can feel like good decisions and accurate understandings. It's the main reason that jumping to conclusions, making false assumptions, and believing faulty logic are so common.

The focus of our attention has a lot to do with our thinking. For instance, when we are intensely focused on an idea or a problem or some activity, we tend not to notice other things around us. To our unconscious minds, it's as if those other things don't even exist.

When we're mentally or physically fatigued, confused, or emotionally aroused, our thinking tends to be less accurate. We're more likely to believe things that we wouldn't otherwise believe, and our thinking gets slower and less precise.

These innate functions and more are all built into our unconscious minds and can affect our thinking, sometimes to our detriment. We can overcome them; rest, willpower, discipline, and focused attention are some of the things we can do to maintain the quality of our thinking, but we need to learn when we're susceptible to these effects and consciously negate them.

Habits of Thinking (Cognitive Habits)

Everything we do that is repetitive becomes unconscious and habitual: automatic. Walking, reading, swinging a golf club, driving a car, answering familiar questions, making familiar assumptions—they all become unconscious with repetition. We can always make them conscious if we want, but why would we? I can think about the way I walk and do it differently if I want, but why would I? I just ignore it and let my unconscious mind control my walking automatically. My conscious mind decides where I want to go, but my unconscious habits move my legs and take me there.

Habits of thinking are a blessing. We couldn't live without them. But sometimes, automatic thinking isn't right for the situation. For instance, we can automatically make a false assumption, which leads to a false conclusion, which leads to a bad decision, which leads to a big mistake…and it all feels right at the moment it's happening. Wouldn't it be better to recognize the possibility for a false assumption and reset the entire process to get a better result? Of course it would.

Some of our habits of thinking are problematic. The most important of these are cognitive biases, and they are the habits that cause us to distort our perceptions of reality, make false assumptions, react emotionally and irrationally, and make faulty assessments about ourselves and others.

Habits of Being (Personality Habits)

Who are you as a person? Are you generous, brave, compassionate, athletic, and honest? Are you timid, a bit loose with the truth, cynical about everything, and something of a loner? Do you avoid confrontation, or are you more aggressive? Are you joyful or grumpy? A good conversationalist? Persuasive? Imaginative?

Your personality is some combination of literally hundreds of traits, and each of those traits is a habitual way that you approach the situations that occur in your life—a habit of being.

Occasionally, like it or not, some of your personality habits can get in your way, bias your thinking, and lead you into momentary lapses—that's when you go stupid. If you're a timid person, for example, you'll see the world as more threatening than it actually is, and your actions will reflect that attitude, even when it isn't warranted. If you're miserly, you'll see everything as disproportionately costly, and you'll probably see others as more greedy than they actually are. If you're an optimist, you'll see things as more positive than they are, and you'll chase down more opportunities than actually exist for you. It's just the opposite if you're pessimistic.

We need to become aware of those times when our personalities are making us think, say, and do things that aren't right for the situations in which we find ourselves.

Habits of being tend to be anchored more deeply in our unconscious minds than habits of thinking, and it's usually more difficult to find the ones that tend to get in our way so that we can adjust them.

Meta Habits

Meta habits are collections of habits of mind that operate together to form higher-level thinking and behavior. In the same way that systems can be aggregated into a hierarchy of higher- and lower-level systems, so can our unconscious habits of mind. In fact, a habit of mind is literally a system within the mind.

Think again of the automobile analogy. An automobile is a system for transporting people and things, with additional uses for signaling the status of its owner and providing pleasurable experiences. An automobile also comprises lower-level systems, such as the engine, the brakes, the steering system, instrumentation, the frame, the body, and more. In that context, the automobile is a meta system: a collection of lesser systems. The human body likewise is a meta system with many lesser systems, such as the skeleton, the circulatory system, the nervous system, digestive system, immune system, each of which also contains even lower-level systems.

In this book, I will focus on three meta habits, Core Purpose, Strategic Thinking, and Strategic Creativity. I selected those meta habits because they are important to the overall functioning of the mind and its ability to shape your life.

Dealing with Our Complexity

The Model of the Mind diagram simplifies it all and makes it look linear—first this, then that, one step at a time. But, as we have seen, it's not simple, and it's not linear. How can we sort it all out? We can't. The brain and its emergent child, the mind, are far too complex, and almost all of that complexity happens unconsciously, below our awareness, in the goldfish bowl.

But when we identify and adjust one thing at a time—one cognitive habit or one personality habit—our brains absorb that one habit and automatically integrate it into the swirling mass of bioelectrochemical activity that gives rise to our minds. We shift our thinking and our behavior a little or a lot, however much we are willing to take on. Soon we find that our mental lapses occur much less often, that our thought processes routinely generate clarity and accuracy, and that we're thinking, saying, and doing the right things at the right times.

The rest of this book will help you use this model of the mind to help you overcome your own version of the goldfish bowl and to upgrade your mind so that you can build the mind power that will lead to more success, better relationships, and a richer life.

COGNITIVE HABITS
(HABITS OF THINKING)

CHAPTER THREE

The Most Common Cognitive Biases and How to Overcome Them

The Downside of Cognitive Habits

Why don't we always see the world as it really is? Why is our Reality B often flawed or incomplete? It's because our cognitive biases cause us to see what we expect to see, what we want to see, what someone else tells us to see, what we saw before, or what we believe we should see. What we *perceive* as reality, accurately or not, is the result of our conditioning, and it's what we deal with as if it were *true* reality.

For instance: A police officer sees a young man running from the scene of a crime, assumes he's the culprit, and arrests the young man. In reality, the young man had nothing to do with the crime and was merely running to catch a bus. The police officer, not noticing the bus, made a false assumption because of unconscious habits of thinking that were based on his years of experience. Normally that experience serves the police officer well, but this time, it didn't. The officer filtered what he saw through his habits of thinking, created an inaccurate Reality B, and acted on that perception, believing his perception to be the actual reality. In the mind of the officer, the young man *was* the criminal, but in reality, he wasn't. Reality B didn't match Reality A.

Another example: In a recent political campaign in the USA, one of the leading candidates, known for her tough-mindedness and icy demeanor, was moved to tears when responding to a question from a reporter. Because it was such a departure from her normal behavior, it was widely reported in the press. One television commentator said while the candidate was a convincing actress, she was disgusting and phony because she was pretending to be deeply moved in order to be more sympathetic to the voters. "Crying for votes" said the commentator contemptuously. Another commentator said the candidate displayed her passion and commitment by revealing the depth of her caring for the first time in public. No one knows the reality behind her emotional response, perhaps not even the candidate herself. However, the two commentators and millions of others created in their minds perceptions of reality, and they cast their votes on the basis of a Reality B that didn't match up with Reality A.

You can see how people who unconsciously distort reality through their habits of thinking put themselves in a position to create false realities and then behave as if their false realities were true.

The Most Common Cognitive Biases

There are hundreds if not thousands of different habits of thinking we use to screen and interpret reality. Among them are hundreds of cognitive biases, which are the problematic habits that so often lead us into going stupid. We can't deal with all of them, but we don't have to. If we focus our attention on the most common ones, we cover 90 percent of the problem.

In this chapter, I briefly introduce you to the most common cognitive biases, and I also tell you about the way to deal with them. You can solve the problem by replacing all your cognitive biases with one single productive habit of thinking, which I call the 2Q habit (2Q = two questions). In the subsequent chapters, I discuss each of the biases in detail with guidance for using the 2Q habit to overcome them.

The Most Common Cognitive Biases

Limiting Beliefs—When flawed beliefs get in our way

Generalization and Simplification—When we generalize and simplify the reality out of a situation

Cause and Effect—When timing and coincidence are liars, and assumptions lead us astray

Either/Or—When we ignore the spectrum of possibilities and assume false dichotomies

Coherence and Pattern Recognition—Making sense of nonsense (even when it really is nonsense), perceiving things that aren't really there, and our internal What You See Is All There Is (WYSIATI) database

The Confirmation Bias; Expectations and Selective Perceptions—

Emotions—The upside and downside of our passions

Projection and the Me-Bias—When *your* reality isn't *my* reality. Are we really as good (or bad) as we think we are? (with special attention to the Dunning-Kruger Effect)

Focus Blindness and Stress—When there's more to the story that we need to know (our unconscious minds don't always see what's there to be seen)

Jumping to Conclusions—How to avoid the "three steps to stupid"

The Duality of Experience—Is the past really a guide to the future? Are our internal experiences real?

Becoming Aware of Your Biases

Awareness is the necessary first step. You can't avoid a bias if you don't know it exists within you, and most of us aren't aware of our biases. By the way, the fact that most of us don't believe we distort reality is itself an example of how we distort reality. If you think you're the exception, you might be—it's possible—but you almost certainly aren't.

It's a good idea to approach this chapter with openness. Even if you're pretty sure you don't experience cognitive biases, try to be open to the possibility. And even in those times when you aren't subject to these biases, knowing more about them will help you deal with the cognitive biases of others.

In the following pages, I'm going to ask you to carefully and attentively read about each of the biases and to remember a time when you were biased in that way. If you can't remember ever having that bias, use your imagination and visualize yourself experiencing it. It'll be a superficial version of the actual experience, but by living it in your imagination, you'll be priming yourself to be aware when that bias might influence you in the future so that you can consciously avoid it. And if you actually have experienced that particular bias without knowing it, visualization is a good way to stimulate your awareness.

Priming is a complex function of the mind. Mind science proves that when your unconscious mind has been exposed to an idea, you're more likely to think and behave in alignment with that idea. The more attention you put to understanding the cognitive biases and how they play out in your own mind, the more thoroughly you'll be priming yourself to be aware of them and to eliminate the flawed thinking they create.

So try to keep an open mind, and do your best to remember or imagine yourself experiencing each distortion as you read about it.

Eliminating Biases: The 2Q Habit

When you've primed yourself to be aware of your potential cognitive biases, what can you do about them? You have to create a new habit of thinking, a replacement habit that causes you to want to understand the situation better and to be open to other possibilities. That, in turn, will stock your unconscious mind with more and better information and enable it to come up with a Reality B that's a much closer match with Reality A. You can do that by asking yourself two questions and then answering each to the best of your ability. The questions are these: What's Reality A?, and What are the possibilities?

- *What's Reality A?*

  What are the facts? What do you *know* is the actual reality outside of your mind (Reality A), and separately, what is the product of your opinion or interpretation (Reality B)? What do you believe that could be questioned?

  Initially, when you ask this question, it'll be hard to distinguish between Reality A and Reality B because all your life, you've been conditioned to perceive and depend upon Reality B as if it were the actual reality rather than an internal perception. But with practice, you'll not only get good at it, you'll also learn automatically to distinguish between them.

- *What Are the Possibilities?*

  What else do you need to know about the situation? What are the other possibilities, even the unlikely ones? How would someone else see the situation?

Your mindset when asking yourself these questions is important. You'll need to adopt the mindset of an objective third party—an impartial observer. In other words, see yourself and your thinking from the point of view of someone who's not involved. It's tricky at first because our minds want to justify what we think we know rather than challenge it or see it differently. So resist the temptation to justify what you think is true, and dig deeper to see if it really is true or not.

Like all new habits, consciously asking yourself the two questions will feel awkward and slow at first. But stick with it because it'll gradually establish itself as an automatic, instant, and, yes, unconscious, habit of mind. After a while—probably several days, maybe a week or so—you'll no longer even have to think about the questions because your mind will no longer need them. You'll have generated the habit of making sure you've seen reality the way it is by automatically increasing the range of possibilities that come to mind and by having the automatic urge to understand the situation as thoroughly as possible.

At that point, it will no longer be the two-question habit; it will be a natural inclination to be aware of all possibilities and to be curious about them.

To genuinely ask "What is Reality A?" and "What are the possibilities?" accomplishes a couple of things. First, it interrupts the automatic operation of your cognitive biases and stimulates conscious thinking. Second, it opens you up to a broader range of possibilities, gets you looking for other points of view, helps you be more objective, and engages your imagination and creativity. The habit of asking the two questions itself becomes habitual in a productive way, and eventually even the two questions fall away because you will have genuinely become a more open, objective, and creative person.

All of this can be a lot of work. And it can be challenging because it's one of those things that's inherently awkward, at least in the beginning. Your mind is enormously complex, and it's taken you all of your lifetime to this point to build the habits of mind that inhabit your head, including the ones that sometimes make you go stupid—the ones that are part of your goldfish bowl. It won't take you a lifetime to release your cognitive biases and establish better habits, but it will take some time, and you have to *engage* in the process or it won't work.

It's not positive thinking, it's not fake it until you make it, it's not slogans or formulas, and it's not opening yourself up to the universe to make things right. It's you reshaping your mind.

If "be all you can be" has any meaning for you (as it does for me), that's what it is.

The 2Q Habit Is the Path Back to Original Mind

How can you regain your Original Mind? You can't. Not really. And you wouldn't want to. True Original Mind is actually pretty mindless. It only exists when you are unformed, thoughtless, and pathetically helpless. You wouldn't want to go back to that state of being, and you couldn't even if you tried.

The components of Original Mind—openness, objectivity, and creativity—are supremely valuable. If the mature you could recover the kind of openness you had as a newborn, you would have access to a whole new world of possibilities. If you could return to complete objectivity, your perceptions of the world and yourself would be unclouded by biases, mistaken beliefs, distorted ideas about yourself, and emotions. You'd again be able to see things as they actually are, at least to the degree that your senses could make them available to you. If you could return to unfettered creativity, you would no longer block, distort, or bias your ability to see the possibilities that will help you steer your way into your most meaningful future.

A mature form of Original Mind—one that is augmented by experience and judgment—will firmly ground your mind in reality, focus your beliefs on what's true, free you from the tyranny of your emotions, and put you on the threshold of wisdom. It'll free you from the many traps of cognitive biases, and, best of all, going stupid will become a rare thing for you.

And there's more good news: this book is already putting you on the path back to Original Mind. The mere fact that you are interested in knowing your mind and yourself better puts you on the first steps of the path. Learning how your mind behaves moves you along that path. Being able to identify and recondition your questionable habits of mind increases your momentum. And if you stick with it, sooner rather than later, you'll be in that state of adult Original Mind that will clean up your thinking, which will clean up your behavior, which will have the kind of impact that you dream of when you dare dream of a better life.

If you do nothing more than adopt the 2Q habit—and stick with it—that alone will open up your Original Mind. If you persist over time, the conscious application of the two-question discipline transforms itself into a productive unconscious habit of thinking. Ultimately that habit of thinking goes deeper and transforms into several habits of being. You become a more curious, receptive (yet discerning), impartial, and resourceful human being in charge of your emotions rather than the other way around, and you'll be known to all for the clarity of your thinking and the wisdom of your actions.

Isn't that what you want?

The Most Common Biases, Up Close and Personal

With that preparation behind us, let's take a close look at each of the cognitive biases. Remember, as you read about each bias, it's important to go through the three-step process:

- Read about each cognitive bias carefully. Understand it.

- Remember or imagine that you have experienced that particular bias. Stay objective as if you were merely an observer.

- Ask and answer the two questions to expand your understanding of that situation and to expose yourself to a broader range of alternatives.

What is Reality A?

What are the possibilities?

CHAPTER FOUR

Limiting Beliefs

Belief that something can't be done—that someone can't be persuaded, that you lack some talent or skill, that the odds are against you, that you'll make a fool of yourself, that a risk is too great, and on and on—limit your effectiveness. The belief might be true, it might be self-fulfilling, or it might just be hogwash.

There are also such things as enabling beliefs: the belief that something *can* be done, someone *can* be persuaded, that you *have* a needed talent or skill, that the odds *are* in your favor, that you'll do a *great* job, that the risk is minimal, etc.

Limiting beliefs and enabling beliefs aren't just a matter of "If you think you can or if you think you can't, you're right." If they were, you would only have to believe to make something possible. It's only when the belief reflects reality or when the belief is so strong that it leads to effective behavior that it leads to effectiveness and success (enabling beliefs) or ineffectiveness and failure (limiting beliefs). Belief alone accomplishes nothing. Rational belief followed by *effective behavior* leads to success. And by rational belief, I mean belief that is consistent with Reality A.

That's why affirmations, false bravado, positive thinking, and other attempts at creating enabling beliefs so often lead to frustration, embarrassment, and ultimately failure. If you don't really believe them consciously or unconsciously or if they're not realistic, they won't be useful, in fact, they'll probably be dysfunctional.

In summary, when there is no congruence between your beliefs and Reality A, the beliefs will be limiting. When the beliefs dovetail with reality—Reality A—and you really do believe them, both consciously and unconsciously, they will be enabling beliefs.

Let me emphasize two forms of limiting beliefs that bedevil most of us:

Self-Perceptions

Self-perception is your conscious and unconscious sense of yourself. You might be surprised by the latter, but your unconscious sense of yourself, probably even more than your conscious self-image, impacts your effectiveness and therefore contributes to your success or lack of it. But because it's unconscious, it can have a hidden impact on you.

Here are some examples that illustrate how self-perceptions can shape behavior, not always for the best.

- *Ted comes from a poor family. He remembers that his mother would never go to an upscale restaurant, not even when he offered to take her for Mother's Day or her birthday. She used to say, "I don't belong in a place like that."*

  The mother's self-image was that of a lower-class person without the necessary standing and social skills to behave appropriately in upper-class situations.

- *What a disaster. My boss, Jack, and I went to our first working meeting with a new client. We were meeting the CEO of a Fortune 500 company. Jack walked in like he owned the place, and started taking charge from the first minute. You could see the client's face turn to stone. Man, was I embarrassed.*

Jack's actual self-image was that of a pretender. He often worried that his clients might discover that he was merely an Average Joe who, by luck, had reached a position of influence and power. To cover up his sense of inferiority, he tried to act like the smartest guy in the room, someone who was a take-charge mover and shaker and who automatically commanded the respect of even the most powerful executives. Because it wasn't consistent with reality, it was never authentic, and the people around him could sense it.

- *Can you believe it? I offered Manny a promotion into sales from market research with great pay, a title, responsibility, an expense account, and even a company car. He said no! When I asked why, he said, "I'm a numbers guy, not a salesman. I can't do that kind of work." It's a shame because he has the ability. You should see him win over skeptical clients when he presents his market research reports.*

Manny's self-image was exactly what he said it was in spite of the fact that he had demonstrated to others his persuasive skills.

- *Sharon is a natural; three days on the job, and she's already a hero. We were about to lose our biggest customer to a competitor who offered a lowball price. Sharon overheard me worrying about it and asked if she could try to turn him around. You should have seen her. She's only three years out of college, but you'd have thought she was a twenty-year veteran. Within a half hour, she put together a service package that brought the customer back, and she didn't even have to cut our price!*

Sharon has the self-image of a winner. She believes that she can turn around even the most difficult of situations, and experience has supported her belief.

- *I don't back down from anyone! If you give me a hard time, be prepared for trouble.*

  This person believes himself to be a forceful, intimidating person who will prevail in most situations, somebody who will be a problem for those who oppose him. But there are many situations that don't react well to such aggressive behavior.

- *The smartest person in the room is Rebecca, but you wouldn't know it. She never speaks up in meetings, and you have to pry opinions and recommendations out of her. But when you do, she always has something worthwhile to contribute.*

  Rebecca's self-mage is that of a worker bee who has no leadership potential. She knows she's smart but sees herself as a person who is not respected or listened to by others. In truth, she is highly respected, but her self-perception focuses on the very few instances in which she spoke up but her ideas were not accepted, leaving her feeling foolish and inept. Those few instances loom large in her mind, giving rise to a false perception of herself or, more accurately, a self-fulfilling perception.

Your self-perceptions don't have to be positive or negative. They simply have to be accurate and based on reality, not on a desire to impress yourself or anyone else.

Self-perception needs to be consistent with your true nature; otherwise, you'll take on tasks for which you're not well suited, you'll give the appearance of being a phony when your behavior doesn't match your assertions about yourself, or you'll resent others when they describe you in ways that seem wrong to you. Basically, an honest, accurate self-image supports effective behavior.

I'm well aware of the prevailing belief that you should fake it until you make it, in other words, act a certain way, and in time, you'll become that way. For instance, take on a positive attitude even if you don't feel positive, and keep doing it. The theory is that eventually, with attention and repetition, you'll actually become innately positive, and the habit of mind of being positive will become ingrained.

But the unconscious mind can be tricky. Faking it until you make it only works if you actually believe it or are at least consciously and unconsciously open to the possibility. If you truly disbelieve it, even unconsciously, you'll initially act the part, but with repetition, instead of integrating the habit of *being* positive, you'll integrate the habit of *acting* positive without becoming truly positive. The behavior of *appearing* positive will become habitual, but the actual personality trait of *being* positive won't. Do you see the difference? Acting shapes your outward behavior, but not your thinking, but an innate positive attitude shapes everything about you.

The unconscious mind is complex and subtle—and *very* smart. It knows when you're faking it. It's important to create new habits that are compatible with who you are so that the resulting new habits will be authentic. If they're not authentically you, they won't shift your thinking, and your old mental habits will persist. You may look outwardly the way you want to look, but inwardly you won't really change. Yet at a conscious level, you'll think you have. In actuality, all you'll have done is to create a new behavioral habit—faking it but never quite making it. While your outward behavior may shift a bit, your unconscious thinking remains in place.

Here's an example of someone whose self-perception changed for the better. Let's call him Jason.

> *Jason struggled for a decade and a half in the banking industry. He had an MBA from a top-ranked school and great leadership training from his military experience. His self-image was that of a person with tremendous upward potential, a corporate achiever who would go far. He was described as brilliant, creative, and resourceful. But his performance evaluations were mediocre, his promotions few and far between. Eventually, he was laid off and landed a job as a management consultant where he did better, yet he still didn't succeed as he thought he should. Ultimately, quite by accident, he was offered a position as an adjunct professor at*

a respected second-tier university. He loves it, and he's good at it. He's thriving. The academic environment plus the opportunity to do groundbreaking research tapped precisely into his strengths and gave him a greater sense of accomplishment and fulfillment than he had ever had before.

Jason's long-standing self-perception was a false one—a distortion of reality—and it led him to make poor choices and career decisions until he fell by accident into exactly the right career path for him. He could have made much more productive use of fifteen years of his life if he had had an accurate self-perception during that time.

The challenge is to bring your unconscious self-perceptions into your conscious awareness and to be rigorously honest with yourself *about* yourself. If you're aware of your self-perceptions, you can do a reality check on yourself by applying the 2Q technique. You simply apply the questions to your own belief about yourself, and, if you're honest, you may be able to identify some self-perceptions that aren't accurate. For instance, a lot of people believe they're outstanding sales people, yet wonder why their sales often fall short of their goals. A close look at themselves, guided by the two questions, can reveal a lot.

Still, self-perceptions can be difficult to uncover, and beliefs about ourselves difficult to dislodge, even when false. In Chapter Sixteen, A Process for Self-Discovery, we'll explore a method for uncovering personality traits that may impede your success, and following that, I'll show you what you can do about them.

Persistence of Belief

Even when proven wrong about a firmly held opinion, the majority of people will persist in believing the opinion, especially if the opinion is based on personal experience, a trusted source of information, or a strong desire. Psychologists have documented this effect, and we easily see it in others. We rarely see it in ourselves.

For example, take the case of generic aspirin. Millions of people buy name-brand aspirin such as Bayer or Anacin, but generic unbranded aspirin costs a third to a half less *for exactly the same product.* Try to convince the brand loyalists that the generic aspirin is exactly the same, show them studies, show them the ingredient labels on the packages, and they still insist that branded aspirin is better and worth the added cost. If you're one of those people, you're undoubtedly shaking your head at my stupidity as you read this paragraph.

Persistence of belief creates two kinds of problems for you. Your own persistence of belief can lead you to make faulty decisions. You need to make a conscious practice of keeping your mind open to the possibility that your opinions, beliefs, biases, and assumptions might not be accurate or might not be a reflection of reality. You don't have to accept or agree with new or alternative ideas, but you need to be open to them; you need at least to consider them.

Dealing with the persistent false beliefs of others can be a frustrating, exasperating experience. With your own persistence of belief, at least you're in control. You can consciously look at other ideas, and be open to them. Even if you disagree with the ideas, you can make an effort to understand them so that you can understand the people who believe in them. You may never be able to shift other people from their false but deeply and sincerely held beliefs. Even when believers are exposed to irrefutable evidence it's common for them to cling to their false beliefs.

If you are to maximize your effectiveness, you must be ready to abandon cherished or strongly held beliefs when credible evidence shows those beliefs to be in error. And you must be more discerning so that you adopt reality-based beliefs in the first place.

Whenever one of your strongly held beliefs is challenged, pause to use the two-question technique to look at the reality of your belief with fresh eyes and to open up to other possibilities. If you have no time in the moment, take a few moments later to review the situation and apply the two questions. You'll either confirm your belief, or you won't, but either way, you'll have a deeper understanding of the situation and your Reality B will be a better representation of Reality A.

CHAPTER FIVE

Generalization and Simplification

Generalizations and simplifications such as anecdotal thinking, stereotyping, demographics, statistics, and overviews of complex subjects are all useful ways of thinking, and they are sometimes the only way we can understand a situation. But be alert. You need stay aware that generalization and simplification can strip the reality out of some situations.

Anecdotes and Anecdotal Evidence

An anecdote is a brief story, true or fictional, that makes a point. Anecdotal evidence is the use of a single incident or a small number of incidents as proof of a broader truth. Anecdotes and anecdotal evidence are useless for analysis and drawing general conclusions, but they're excellent for communicating in a way that captures the audience's attention.

Anecdotes can distort your thinking if you generalize from them. An anecdote represents a single incident and is representative of that incident only. That's why anecdotal evidence is so flawed; it represents one or a small number of incidents, not a general truth. Here's a tasteless and extreme (but true) illustration:

> *In the year 2005, a human finger was found in a salad at a Wendy's fast-food restaurant. It was a one-time incident. In all of Wendy's thousands of restaurants, and indeed in all of the more than one hundred thousand fast-food restaurants of all kinds, this had never*

happened before. Because it was such a lurid event, the news media publicized it repeatedly over a period of weeks, and the public was repelled by the thought of a severed human finger in a salad.

The odds of any one customer finding something this repulsive in his or her food was on the order of a billion to one, much less of a chance than winning the lottery. Yet based on this single piece of anecdotal evidence, many thousands of customers who otherwise liked Wendy's restaurants and food stayed away.

In this case, the anecdote carried a high emotional charge—disgust, revulsion, and maybe a bit of fear. People didn't think about the reality of the situation and the very low odds of having such an experience. They reacted emotionally to the event and associated a sense of disgust with Wendy's. You may remember that the finger incident was a fraudulent attempt to extort money from Wendy's by way of the courts, and, in fact, no one had ever actually suffered such an incident. It never happened. Yet Wendy's business suffered.

If you know what the reality of a situation is, anecdotes can be an excellent way to communicate it; anecdotes are simple stories that can personalize and add energy and emotion to your communications. I use them frequently in this book to illustrate key points. My anecdotes don't prove anything, but because each of them actually does represent a general truth, they serve as a good way to make the broader underlying points, which have proven to be true based on other valid sources.

An unethical but legal use of anecdotes is to present one or a few true cases, saying or implying that those cases represent a general truth when in fact they don't. For instance, a recent advertisement for a weight-loss supplement said something like, "Mary Sue Ralston of Avoirdupois, Louisiana, lost sixty-seven pounds on the Schlimm diet." No doubt Mary Sue truly did lose that weight on that diet, but the commercial didn't say that she also cut down on the amount of food she ate and stuck to a regular plan of exercise. It also didn't say what percentage of people who tried the Schlimm diet were successful in losing weight and keeping it off. Mary Sue's experience was true for her, but it didn't necessarily reflect a general truth.

Another commercial for a well-known brand of pickup truck stated something like, "Sam Peck of Bighat, Texas, has been driving his truck for two hundred fifty thousand miles and expects another one hundred thousand." The implication is that your experience with that brand of trucks will be the same as Sam Peck's, even though the actual mileage statistics for that brand of truck aren't mentioned. Again, Sam's experience, even if true, doesn't necessarily reflect a broader truth.

Don't accept anecdotal evidence as representative of a broader reality unless you know the broader reality actually is true. Anecdotes are only representative of the events they describe. Also, anecdotes can be a great way to add emotion and persuasive power to your communications, but remember that it's unethical to assert that the anecdote represents the general reality if, in fact, it doesn't.

Stereotypes

Stereotyping occurs when we assume individuals have the same characteristics we associate with a group of similar people. But often, these characteristics don't extend to individuals within that group. The danger in stereotyping is that you might attribute common characteristics of a class of people to an individual who fits that class and thus do injustice to the individual.

Do you know any people of Irish descent? Are they alcoholics? Do you know any Muslims? Are they terrorists? Are all MBA graduates outstanding managers? Are all senior citizens forgetful? Are all teenagers poor drivers? Do all redheads have hot tempers? Are all Scots thrifty? Are all homeless people lazy? Are all mothers-in-law obnoxious? Are all Chinese-Americans great students? Are all fat people jolly?

Of course not.

Individuals are not stereotypes. If we are to deal with them effectively, we must deal with them as individual people, not as we think most of them are. When we deal with individuals, we find that there are sober Irishmen, law-abiding Muslims, MBAs who mismanage, senior citizens who aren't forgetful, expert teenaged drivers, calm redheads, spendthrift Scots, industrious homeless people, loveable mothers-in-law, stupid Chinese-Americans, and ill-tempered fat men.

Stereotypes are useful. They give us hints about what we *might* find in people, and they help entrepreneurs, politicians, universities, and other organizations serve large populations, but each individual is his/her own person and should be dealt with individually. Look for the stereotype in each person if you want to, but be prepared to see something else, and always deal with people based on their specific characteristics, not their stereotypes.

Before I started writing this book, the first two women in history graduated from the U.S. Army's rigorous Ranger School. I paid close attention because I myself graduated from Ranger School many years ago. The event was controversial and caused a lot of discussion in the news media, and stereotyping was at the heart of it. I heard comments suggesting women don't belong in combat roles because they are a danger to themselves and those around them, women don't have the physical strength to overcome the demands of Rangers in combat, women aren't temperamentally suited for Ranger duty, and on and on. Those opinions may be true for many if not most women. But at least these two women proved that the stereotype wasn't true for them. Fortunately, the army decided to allow people into Ranger School based on their qualifications, not their stereotypes. The news reported that twenty women entered that Ranger class, and only two graduated. So the stereotype held mostly true, but wouldn't it have been an injustice for the army to deny all women access to Ranger School even if they were qualified for it? Ditto police work, ditto firefighting, and, at one time, ditto the right to vote.

Demographics and Statistics

You can survey and demographically define the average American, but you probably can't find a single person who exactly fits the statistical profile of an average American. If the average American is 5'5", weighs 173 pounds, is 42 years old, earns $52,300 per year, and is married with 1.5 children, that's useful information (I made those numbers up, so don't take them as gospel). But I'll bet you don't know a single person who fits that profile. It might be accurate for the population, yet it describes almost no individual. Yet the idea of the average American is a useful idea in a broad, general way. If I ask you to tell me about the average teenager and the average senior citizen, or if I ask you to compare the typical Democrat with the typical Republican, or doctors compared with glass blowers, you can say some meaningful things about each group, can't you? That's the value of demographics and statistics. Even when you don't use numbers to describe them, you have some ideas about them (stereotypes), and those ideas help you understand the world we live in, don't they? They make a hugely complex world more understandable.

But watch out. Even when they consist of general impressions rather than statistical analyses, demographics are a form of stereotyping when you apply them to individuals. Individuals almost always differ in important ways from the stereotypes or statistical models that describe them.

Yes, believe it or not, demographic studies—and the statistics that underlie them—are a form of stereotyping and a very useful form indeed. We conduct studies in which we ask individual people questions about themselves and their behavior, and we use statistical formulas to draw conclusions about these groups.

By the way, have you noticed that the responses people make to survey questionnaires are anecdotes? And as such, they're only true for the individuals. Yet when we collect large numbers of them, they become statistics. When do anecdotes become statistics? When the numbers are large enough that we can conclude that they are representative of the larger group. The only difference between anecdotal evidence and statistical evidence is the number of observations. Is one anecdote (or questionnaire in a survey) representative of a population? No. How about two? Still no. How about ten? Well, maybe. It depends on the size of the population. How about a hundred? Again, it depends on the size of the population of the group. There's a lot of gray area, isn't there? That's what the science (and science it truly is) of statistics deals with. Statistics don't do away with gray areas; statistics help us understand them.

We can draw a lot of very useful conclusions based on demographics and statistics. We use those conclusions to make important decisions about marketing strategies, political campaigns, product designs, medical treatments, social theories, government laws and regulations, crime fighting tactics, financial policies, tax rates, college admissions, and any number of other ways of dealing with large groups of people. It's useful and appropriate to use demographics and statistics to deal with groups of people and institutions because that's really the only way to understand them as groups. Without demographics and the statistics that underlie them, understanding large groups of people and complex systems would be darn near impossible.

Yet that large truth breaks down when dealing with individuals and very small groups. You can never draw valid conclusions about individuals by assuming that statistics (including demographics and nonnumerical generalizations like stereotypes) are true of them. You'll only be right occasionally and by accident, and you'll be wrong a whole lot more than you'll be right. If your Reality B about an individual person is based on statistics or stereotypes, your Reality B will often be wrong or only partly right at best. When you're dealing with individuals—whether you're a salesperson, police officer, medical doctor, or just you and me—you absolutely *must* understand them individually and deal with them as the specific individuals they are and not as stereotypes and generalities. If you don't, you're deliberately divorcing yourself from the reality of the individual, and that leads to injustice and stupid decisions.

Have you ever telephoned or emailed a large business? Was it a pleasant experience? Not likely. You were probably treated as if you were the average customer (a statistical stereotype) with a predetermined set of needs rather than the individual you are. You probably had to thread your way through a bunch of screening questions designed to categorize you into one of the predetermined problem solutions that research indicates are needed for the target market. You may or may not have ever reached an actual human being, and if you did, that human being was trained to treat you the way the research says the average customer should be treated, including extremely polite (but artificial) treatment and a chipper demeanor that probably seemed rehearsed rather than authentic. You were probably treated to standard responses to the questions you were expected to ask (because those are the questions the average customer would ask). And if your questions or problems weren't exactly as the person or system was programmed to deal with, you were met with confusion. Maybe the system finally solved your problem or answered your question (after it made you jump through a lot of hoops and frustrated you). If it didn't (and if you were lucky), you were passed on to someone who had the authority to deal with you as an individual. Or maybe you simply gave up in exasperation.

In business (or politics, medicine, education, or whatever), when you assume that individual people are the same as the demographic profile of all people, that's when you get into trouble. As you already know, too many organizations, especially large ones whose managers are far removed from their clientele, train their employees to deal with the average client. In doing so, they condition their employees' unconscious minds with the impression that when they're dealing with you, they're dealing with a stereotype, not an individual human being.

That's the danger of demographics and statistics; they tend to condition you, mostly unconsciously, to see individual people as demographics and statistics rather than the individuals they truly are. Yes, the demographics and statistics help you manage an organization efficiently, but if you're not careful, those same demographics and statistics bias you to see individuals in ways that aren't realistic, in ways that alienate them, and in ways that deny them the personal attention that will serve their needs and yours.

KISS (Keep It Simple, Stupid)

One of the most time-honored guidelines we have for efficiency is KISS—keep it simple, stupid. And it works great, except when it doesn't, and then you can go all kinds of wrong.

Believe it or not, simplicity itself is a complex subject.

First of all, your mind, consciously and unconsciously, craves simplicity. Brain scans and carefully controlled experiments repeatedly show that the mind understands simple ideas more readily than complex ones. No surprise there, but the mind also more readily accepts simple ideas as true even when they're not. We accept simple explanations for complex phenomena because, unconsciously, simplicity *feels* better; it feels more *true* than something complex. Your intuition tells you that simple is true even when it's not. Why? Simple ideas are easy to understand. They require less mental focus and less memory. They generate fewer negative emotions such as anxiety and frustration and more positive emotions such as satisfaction and that comfy sensation we get when we think we understand something important. Your mind likes that, prefers that, and believes that. A false aha feels just as good as a true aha to the unconscious mind.

So we're geared to accept and to believe the simple version of things; we're wired for simplicity.

Problem: the modern world is a complex place. Reality A is often complex, and when we believe a Reality B that's simple, when it's really not, we're getting it wrong even though it feels so right.

My point is not that we should avoid making decisions when we lack complete understanding of the situation or the consequences of our decisions. We can't always understand the consequences, and the more complex the situation, the less we understand the outcomes of our decisions. We need to be aware of our desire, our *need*, to simplify, to know when we're doing it, and to *stop* doing it.

When we recognize the complexity of a situation, or its simplicity if it is indeed simple, we can make decisions with a full sense of the certainty or uncertainty of the outcome. We can stop creating false expectations and allow for "I don't know." We can eliminate many of our biases because we're more open to all possible outcomes rather than seeing a narrow range of outcomes based on false or distorted expectations. We can become more open to seeing the situation as it unfolds and adjusting to it rather than insisting that everything is okay until failure smacks us in the face.

It's not easy to resist our need for simplicity because it exposes us to uncertainty, and as much as the mind craves simplicity, it rejects uncertainty. In fact, as you'll see later in the chapter on coherence and pattern recognition, the mind's coherence function creates a sense of certainty, even when it's false certainty. So your conscious mind needs to overcome two innate urges: its need to simplify when the situation is complex and its need for certainty when your Reality B is not certain.

The two questions pull you out of your desire for simplicity and put you into a inquiring frame of mind, a mindset in which you're more likely to perceive the actuality of the situation, whether simple or complex.

CHAPTER SIX

Cause and Effect

When things coincide in time or location, our unconscious impulse is to assume cause and effect. We rarely pause to call on our conscious thinking to determine whether it actually is cause and effect, merely coincidence, or that we simply don't know one way or the other.

Consider this familiar scenario:

> *I caught a cold on an airplane yesterday. Today, I have a cold, and yesterday, I was breathing all that stale air from the other passengers, so of course that's where I caught the cold.*

Really? Or was it merely a coincidence, and there was actually no connection between your cold and the airplane ride? Is there any way to know for sure? No. But the mind saw a connection, probably fueled by some beliefs about catching colds, and it concocted the story about catching cold on an airplane. It may or may not be true. We just don't know.

Here's another scenario:

> *In a community north of San Francisco, there's a controversy involving inoculations, injections of medicine intended to make children immune to certain diseases, such as whooping cough, or polio, or others. A lot of families in that area believe that inoculations can cause autism in children because, in fact, some children*

actually were diagnosed with autism after being inoculated. These concerned parents assume cause and effect—inoculations cause autism—and won't allow their children to be inoculated. The concerned parents understand that this puts their children at risk for whooping cough or other diseases, but they believe that autism represents a far greater risk, so no inoculation for their kids.

It all sounds pretty reasonable, doesn't it?

But there's another side that insists inoculations have nothing to do with autism. They believe that autism developed in some kids simply as a result of the normal occurrence of autism in a population. There are bound to be some kids who got inoculated and also developed autism, but one had nothing to do with the other.

Who's right? Does inoculation cause autism? Or doesn't it? Should kids be inoculated or not?

I don't know how this controversy will ultimately play out, but I do know that it was caused by flawed habits of mind, principally the ones that make us notice a correlation and jump to either the cause and effect conclusion or the coincidence conclusion. Then, having jumped to that conclusion, these parents cling to it as if it were fact. The flaw in the thinking of both sides is the lack of "I don't know" and the insistence on "I do know" even when that stance wasn't justified.

"I know" is a closed mindset; it's not open to new evidence, other points of view, or a wider range of possibilities, and it generates false certainty. "I don't know," on the other hand, is a mindset that encourages a search for new information and better understanding. It's open to other points of view and a wide range of possibilities. And most importantly, "I don't know" doesn't lock you into a rigid conclusion, partial understanding, or a limited range of possibilities.

The awareness you need to cultivate is that there are three, not two, alternatives to consider: cause and effect, coincidence, or "I don't know." The new habit of mind you need to cultivate is this: whenever there is doubt (even minor doubt), controversy (both sides can't be right), or any of those nagging head, heart, or gut signals alerting you that something is off, you need to consciously adopt the "I don't know" mindset or even the mindset that says, "I think I know, but I'm not certain, so I need to be open to other possibilities." That'll keep you open to more information, a wider range of possibilities, and other points of view, and it'll make you a better decision-maker.

The two-question technique interrupts your false certainty and superficial thinking and puts you into a state of "I don't know" (even when you think you *do* know). The two questions force you to think about other possibilities and to search for more information about a subject.

CHAPTER SEVEN
Either/Or

Let me start this section with a couple of quotes from the book *Born to Believe* by Dr. Andrew Newberg and Mark Waldman:

> The brain has a tendency to reduce everything to as few components as possible. In the hidden recesses of the inferior parietal lobe, there exists a cognitive function that puts abstract concepts into polarized dyads, or dualistic terms....It is easier for the brain to first quantify objects into pairs, and then to differentiate them into opposing groups: light or dark, happy or sad, fact or fiction, good or evil, right or wrong, Republican or Democrat, and so on....Furthermore, once an oppositional dyad is created, the brain will then impose an emotional bias on each part of the dyad. Thus, once we divide objects, people, and ideals into groups, we will tend to express a preference for one and a dislike for the other.

> When individuals are randomly placed into different groups, they feel stronger about their own group and tend to feel negatively about other groups...thus simply being a part of a group results in ill will toward other groups.

Our minds want to simplify things into either/or, them/us, good/bad, happy/sad, winning/losing, and so on. It's a form of dualism. Our minds find it easier to perceive the world in pairs of opposites, so our unconscious minds create perceptions of reality that tend to be dualistic. But the world isn't necessarily a dualistic place. Things don't always come in oppositional pairs. It may seem that way to us because our minds want to construct Reality B that way even when Reality A isn't at all dualistic.

Events are rarely purely good or purely bad. Experiences aren't delightful or miserable; they come in all shades and degrees of happy, sad, and neutral, and often they're an unpredictable mix of all of the above. Groups that don't include us aren't always bad, wrong, or undesirable, and our group (family, club, gang, school, neighborhood, sports team, political party, race, religion, etc.) isn't always good, right, or desirable.

I was listening to a radio talk show the other day, and the host of the show asked the guest, a prominent politician, a question on a complex subject. For our purposes, the question doesn't matter. What matters is that the host insisted that the guest give a yes or no answer to the question. When the guest politely demurred, wanting to give a more complete answer, the host verbally attacked him, saying something like, "Can't you give a simple yes or no answer? Why do you have to be so evasive? What are you afraid of?"

I found myself agreeing with the host for a moment, thinking to myself, "Yeah, why is this bozo being so evasive? What's he hiding?" Then I caught myself. I know full well that the human mind tends to reduce things to simplistic dualisms, yet I had fallen into that very trap, at least for a moment, until my conscious mind asserted itself by triggering my awareness of my own tendency toward dualism.

It's a trap we all fall into unless we sharpen our awareness so that we can alert ourselves when we're doing it and then trigger the two-question habit in order to bring ourselves out of our distortions and back to reality—Reality A, that is.

CHAPTER EIGHT

Coherence and Pattern Recognition

Your Unconscious Mind Is a Coherence Machine

There's a lot of brain/mind science revealing that our minds are coherence machines given to making sense of our world and revealing patterns to us, whether or not our perceptions are accurate or the patterns we perceive actually exist. Usually they do; sometimes they don't. The mind's coherence function is an indispensible ability, and we couldn't survive without it, but as you have seen in this book for other habits of mind, it can sometimes lead us seriously astray.

In my home, we have a painting of a forested mountain seen from the distance of a couple of miles. On the mountain are two side-by-side rock formations about two-thirds up the mountainside. Beneath the rock formations is another rock formation. My mind can't help seeing these formations and their shadows as a face on the mountainside. It's not a face of course, merely rocky shapes and shadows. But my mind's pattern recognition insists on interpreting the configuration on the mountain as the face of a gruff old man. My conscious mind knows better, but my unconscious mind can't help seeing the face and sensing how wrong, how off it is. Mountains don't have faces (except for Mount Rushmore), so I know full well that it's not a face, yet the face-like pattern disturbs my perceptions and ruins what would otherwise be a nice piece of art.

I'm not the only one whose unconscious mind does this. Some years ago, the world was treated to photographs of the surface of the planet Mars. For a few days, the headlines were filled with reports of a human (or near human) face on the planet's surface along with abundant speculation about how such a likeness came to be in a spot where no human or any other form of life had ever existed. You can imagine what speculations fertile minds came up with. The fact is, however, that given the size of the planet and the millions of instances of rocks, drifting sand, and shadows, it would be a surprise if there were no configurations that resembled two paired features (eyes?), a vertically oriented feature (nose?), and another horizontal feature (mouth?) within a crater or upon a mound or other roundish feature (head?).

The face on the mountain and the face on Mars were not imaginary. They were real. But they weren't faces. Our Reality B perceived them as faces, but the Reality A about them is that they were nothing more than randomly occurring rocks, sand, and shadows. Our minds' coherence function—specifically the pattern recognition aspect of the coherence function—convinced many of us that we were seeing a face, not merely shadows and rocks.

My unconscious mind is both an artist and a storyteller, and so is yours. Our minds take what we see and remember and build coherent stories to explain it. We believe these stories because our unconscious minds attach emotional meaning to them and make sure they seem reasonable to us. We're built that way, and in the normal course of events in a familiar world, our perceptions and the stories our unconscious minds tell us about them give us a pretty good sense of the Reality A of our world.

The coherence function of our unconscious minds work, and they work extremely well. We just have to feed them good information so they can feed us good conclusions. But good information is sometimes a problem.

WYSIATI (What You See Is All There Is) and Blind Spots

The unconscious mind operates as if the information it knows is all the information there is—what it knows is all there is to know—but sometimes our unconscious minds get it wrong. Our information is often incomplete or erroneous. Our mental models are sometimes skewed. Our cognitive biases sometimes twist our perceptions from reality to something else, and as a result, our Reality B sometimes doesn't match Reality A.

Nobel Prize laureate Daniel Kahneman in his book *Thinking, Fast and Slow* calls it WYSIATI, the acronym for "what you see is all there is." Think of WYSIATI as your internal database. You're not a computer, but it's a useful analogy.

Our unconscious minds are working fine. All the connections connect as they should, and we're sane and reasonable. But the raw materials of knowledge and mental models plus our various built-in biases are incomplete or flawed, so when our unconscious coherence machines get it wrong, it's not because of a deficiency in our wiring but because of flawed and incomplete information and beliefs. It's the human equivalent of GIGO in computers—garbage in, garbage out. In human terms, it's incomplete or erroneous information in, flawed Reality B out.

The validity of our unconscious thinking depends completely on what information our unconscious mind has available or can generate. The unconscious mind doesn't know what it doesn't know; it has no sense of blind spots or the possibility of additional information. It simply takes what it has, makes sense of it (creates coherence), and delivers the results to our conscious minds. Whether those results reflect Reality A or not, our unconscious minds process it all into our Reality B, for better or worse.

WYSIATI can leave blind spots in our knowledge and awareness. But WYSIATI isn't the only source of blind spots. Sometimes, habits such as generalization, limiting beliefs, cause and effect, the either/or assumption, and the other distortions you'll be reading about in this book can create blind spots and false beliefs that are every bit as distorting to our perception—our Reality B—as a flawed WYSIATI.

It's the consistency (coherence) of the information that matters for a good story, not its completeness. In fact, you'll often find that knowing little makes it easier to fit everything you know into a believable story. The coherence function tends to create such a story, and it suppresses doubt and ambiguity.

It's the job of the conscious mind to be alert for WYSIATI and blind spots in order to seek or at least allow for the possibility of other information and other impressions. Here's the key question: If our coherence functions feed us convincing stories that seem to right to us, and they do it unconsciously, how can we know when they're in error, and what can we do about it?

You'll never know if the conclusions that make up your Reality B are in error unless you consciously examine them and seek more information to confirm or refute them. But life is full of experiences and activities, and who has the time or the willingness to reexamine every experience, every belief, and every impression our minds come up with? Nobody, that's who. Yet we still need to make sure our Reality B is sound and our decisions wise, especially for matters that are important to our lives. The problem is to identify which conclusions supplied by our unconscious minds might be wrong and then either verify them or reshape them into something more accurate.

To do that, we need to learn from brain/mind science to see which stories our minds provide us are most likely to be wrong and to put our attention on those. There are four situations we can use to alert ourselves when to engage the 2Q habit so that our conscious minds can take charge and so that they can feed our unconscious minds better information.

> *Complexity*: As we saw earlier, both our conscious and unconscious minds prefer simple ideas. They generate simplicity even when the reality of the situation is complex, and they find simplicity more believable even when it's false. So when confronted by complexity, when simplicity doesn't feel quite right, or when the situation is important, we need to consciously initiate the two-question technique to verify our thinking, or to reach more thoughtful conclusions and therefore a more accurate Reality B.

> *Uncertainty*: Also, as we saw earlier, our conscious and unconscious thinking prefers certainty; it wants "I know," not "I don't know." So when the situation and/or its outcome are uncertain

or when we know things are uncertain but we still feel a sense of certainty about our actions and conclusions, we need to double-check our sense of certainty by consciously engaging the two-question technique.

Novelty/Unfamiliarity: Our unconscious minds have learned over the course of our lives how to deal with routine, familiar situations, and they do so with remarkable reliability and ease. When we are confronted by surprises and unfamiliar situations, however, our minds try to relate the experience to something familiar in our past and deal with the current situation as if it were similar. So when confronted by surprises and novelty, even when we feel comfortable with our reactions and thoughts, we need to engage the two-question technique, most of all when the situation is important and we can't afford to be wrong.

Off Signals: Our unconscious minds are always at work, and when we encounter situations that conflict with our experience, what we think we know, or our mental models, or when things simply don't make sense, our unconscious minds send us signals—emotional responses, gut feelings, and intuitions—that something isn't right. It's that off feeling that we so often don't pay attention to. Well, when the situation is important, we need to pay attention to the off feeling, whatever form it takes for us, and look more deeply into the situation. Even when feelings of off-ness are subtle and easy to ignore but the consequences are important, we need to engage the two-question technique.

The 2Q habit puts us back on the right path, helps us find the errors made by our coherence machines, and clears up our unconscious thinking.

CHAPTER NINE

The Confirmation Bias: Expectations and Selective Perception

The Confirmation Bias

You've probably heard the term "confirmation bias" and know it means that we pay attention to and interpret information in ways that tend to confirm our existing beliefs. That's only partly right. Confirmation bias works much more unconsciously and insidiously than that.

Here is a paraphrased explanation of confirmation bias from Daniel Kahneman, the Nobel laureate I quote often in this book:

> *Confirmation bias is an innate operation of your unconscious mind. When presented with an idea—a hypothesis—your unconscious mind tests the hypothesis by looking for confirming evidence. It has a positive bias. It tries to believe the hypothesis rather than refute it or take an objective stance. Your unconscious mind is gullible and biased to believe; your conscious mind is in charge of doubting and unbelieving, but it's sometimes focused on other things or has no information that would stimulate disbelief.*

Notice especially this sentence: "Your unconscious mind is gullible and biased to believe; your conscious mind is in charge of doubting and unbelieving." That's why your intuitions and aha moments—which are generated in the unconscious mind—seem so true, so certain, even when they're not.

What do we conclude from this? People notice and believe data that are compatible with the beliefs they currently hold and interpret data in ways that tend to confirm those beliefs. They ignore, rationalize, or simply don't notice data that conflict with their beliefs.

Kahneman also noted that the confirmatory bias of your unconscious mind "... favors uncritical acceptance of exaggerations of the likelihood of extreme and improbable events." For instance, look at one of modern history's most horrific events and the exaggerated impact it has had on our lives since September 11, 2001. The terrorist attacks on US soil and airspace on that date killed roughly four thousand people (about 0.001 percent of the population). Cancer, heart disease, automobile accidents, crime, and a hundred other causes kill far more people. The risk of dying of any of these causes is enormously greater than the risk of dying by terrorist attack. But they're routine, normal, unremarkable. That's Reality A.

But the scene on 9/11 was horrific, and we all continuously saw it on television and in print for weeks. We consciously and unconsciously engraved the horror of it deeply and ineradicably in our minds and memories, and we can still easily evoke the emotions that it stimulated in us. In the years since, our perceptions about terrorists and, by association, Muslims have solidified, and our national policies, if not our very national character, have shifted significantly toward security at the expense of liberty. 9/11 was both extreme and improbable, and it did exactly as Kahneman describes—it engraved itself in our conscious and unconscious minds in extreme ways, coloring our lives like no other event in our lifetimes. That's Reality B for most of us.

Your conscious mind has the power to intercede and override your unconscious confirmation bias, but it's critical you understand that it doesn't do so unless you are aware that you actually are influenced by the confirmation bias. The two-question technique gives you the tool you need to put confirmation bias into its proper perspective.

Expectations

An expectation is an idea of the future that you consciously or unconsciously believe will happen. If your expectations are based on a clear sense of reality and an understanding that the future is uncertain, and if you're open to the negative and positive possibilities, you'll be able to adjust to unexpected situations without much internal distress. You'll be able to deal with the situation effectively.

Problems occur when your expectations aren't based in reality and/or when you get locked into them.

When your expectations are based on a distorted perception of reality and something goes wrong, you're surprised. Your (flawed) sense of reality leads you to think, "This shouldn't be happening. It doesn't make sense," and you thrash around trying to fix the situation or revise your expectations, which are still grounded in a false perception of reality (a flawed Reality B). One of three things happens: (1) you continue to thrash around with growing frustration and diminishing effectiveness, (2) you make decisions that, by chance, lead to the desired result, or (3) you come to the realization that you need to understand the situation better, take steps to do so, and revise your expectations based on a better understanding (a better Reality B). Of course, #3 is what you should have done in the first place.

What happens when you get locked into unrealistic expectations? You're rigidly committed to making the expectation happen despite the problems, interruptions, and frustrations that seem to mysteriously crop up. It doesn't occur to you to challenge your understanding of reality, so you push to achieve the expectations that seem right and realistic. You think it's simply a matter of determination and commitment, so you push and push, all the while puzzled by the inability to get the job done the way it should be done.

The only way out of this dilemma of unrealistic expectations is to develop the awareness that your perception of what's real may be flawed and at the same time develop the ability to be open to other possibilities. That leads to better understanding of reality, which leads to more realistic expectations.

So when the stakes are important, you need to get your expectations right, or at least acknowledge that they're uncertain so that you'll be mentally prepared to adjust and adapt to the emerging situation. The two-question technique will set you on the right path.

And it's not a bad idea to avoid single-minded expectations of any kind and instead be aware of the range of possibilities. Some possibilities will be more probable than others, but if you're aware of all (or most) possibilities, you won't get locked in to a preferred one, and you'll be mentally and emotionally prepared for other outcomes. That way, your thinking will always be open, and you'll adjust more readily to surprises and low-probability outcomes when they occur.

Selective Perception

Selective perception is an interesting variant of expectations and the primary driver of the confirmation bias. Selective perceptions occur when you have expectations about people, events, information, or anything else. If you believe, for instance, that the leader of your country is wise and capable, you will tend to perceive everything he does as right and proper. If you believe he is stupid and incompetent, you will tend to perceive everything he does as bungling and ineffective. In other words, you'll notice what he does that meets your expectations and not notice or rationalize what doesn't match up with your expectations. If, on the other hand, you maintain an open, receptive state of mind about him, you will make objective, realistic assessments of each of his various decisions and actions, and you will have a more realistic sense of his presidency.

People see and understand what they expect to see and understand much more easily than something that doesn't fit with their established ideas or expectations. When you have an expectation, your interpretation of events will tend to reinforce—confirm—the expectation. If you have a particular belief, even if it's a false belief, you will tend to observe the world in ways that are consistent with that belief. If you have a bias, you tend to see things that support your bias. Your mind selects what it prefers and selectively interprets it to conform to your desires and preferences.

There's an interesting and all too common flip side to this coin. When people selectively give out information, they're distorting reality, sometimes deliberately and sometimes unconsciously. When politicians do it, we call it "spin." When marketing people do it, we call it advertising. When you and I do it, we're either called liars, or if we're unconsciously doing it, we're called everything from "mistaken" to "stupid."

When you selectively perceive information and events, you are denying yourself a full understanding of reality. Your resulting decisions and behavior will be flawed, and your effectiveness will be diminished.

First impressions are considered important because they start to create positive or negative selective perceptions. Say you're meeting someone for the first time; if he has a sweaty handshake and won't make eye contact, doesn't that make a poor first impression? Doesn't that affect the way you perceive him from that point on? It's much easier to make a first impression, good or bad, on someone than it is to reverse an impression after it has been made.

CHAPTER TEN

Emotions

Emotions aren't really cognitive biases, but they often distort thinking, reinforce cognitive biases, and cause us to behave in abnormal and dysfunctional ways. In many ways, emotions could be considered the most important of the biases. You can overcome emotional excesses using the 2Q habit, just as you would for a cognitive bias.

What do you do when someone gets angry with you, gets in your face, or makes threats? Do you get angry in response? Do you withdraw to avoid the anger and your own emotional reaction? Do you go numb in confusion? Or do you allow yourself to feel however you feel (i.e., angry, fearful, confused) but force yourself to listen to the message within the anger and behave appropriately to the situation rather than in response to the anger?

The last response is the most effective, of course, but it's not the one that comes naturally to most of us.

Most people react emotionally to emotion directed at them. Usually that's a mistake. Emotions distort your sense of what's real. The stronger the emotion, the greater the distortion. If you're responding emotionally, then you're distorting a reality that was already distorted by the person directing emotions toward you—a double dose of distortion. Malcolm Gladwell makes the point in his best-selling book *Blink*:

> *Have you ever tried to have a discussion with an angry or fright-*
> *ened human being? You can't do it. You might as well try to argue*
> *with your dog.*

> *[Emotional] Arousal leaves us mind-blind. Most of us, under pres-*
> *sure, get too aroused, and past a certain point, our bodies begin*
> *to shut down so many sources of information that we start to*
> *become useless.*

Why are emotions important? Because they're motivators. They're signals of importance. They can add a sense of reality to your mental models even when those models aren't actually realistic. And they can be signals for you to take a closer look at your Reality B. Let me say more about each of these points.

Emotions are motivators, and they can be extremely strong motivators. We've all seen people in a rage doing unthinkable things that they'd never do in less emotional circumstances. We've all seen people in love doing things that don't otherwise make sense. We go to great lengths to relieve and avoid strong negative emotions like fear, anger, and grief and to stimulate and hold on to the strong positive emotions like joy, peace, love, and deep satisfaction. The problem is that when in an emotional state of any kind, we tend to go unconscious unless we insert our awareness into the situation and put our conscious minds in charge.

Emotions are signals of importance. We don't get emotional about trivialities, yet we get very emotional about things of importance. And by "importance," I mean what's important to our conscious and unconscious minds. We've all seen people go off the deep end about something that seems totally inconsequential to us. But to the person in the emotional state, there is importance to the situation whether we see it or not and whether we agree on its importance or not.

And believe it or not, emotions can add a sense of reality to our mental models. For example, I recently returned from a photographic safari in Africa. At one point, our Land Rover vehicle was extremely close to an agitated and nervous bull Cape buffalo. Let me tell you, a Cape buffalo can be a very scary beast. Our guide, who knew about buffalo behavior, told us there was no danger, so I was able to calm myself and enjoy the experience. But another member of our party, I'll call him Harry, was clearly in a state of fear, imagining all the devastating things an enraged Cape buffalo could do to our Land Rover and us. Harry knew beyond a doubt—he absolutely *knew*—that it was going to attack us.

Scientists have learned that strong emotions lend a sense of reality to our thoughts even when they are not based on actual reality. Harry's fear lent his thoughts of devastation from a buffalo attack a sense of reality, so much so that he couldn't accept our guide's assurances and was convinced of the impending disaster. Later, Harry's anger persisted, and even though nothing bad had happened, he accused our guide of endangering us and even wrote a letter to the safari management to complain. Fear made his mental model—in his mind—both real and unshakeable.

Finally, emotions can be an indicator to our conscious minds that something might be out of whack with our Reality B. We get upset when things don't turn out the way we want them to or when people challenge what we know to be true. Upset means emotional, angry, anxious, disappointed, irritated, and even surprised and amazed. Our expectations and our beliefs are based on our view of the world, our Reality B. When something or someone violates our sense of reality, we get upset. That's a signal. Either the something or someone that upset us is wrong and we're right, or we're wrong, or both. Either way, it's wise to consciously check in and verify our own sense of reality. To do that, we need to be open to the possibilities, some of which might challenge our beliefs. We shouldn't assume that our idea of reality is right, but we also shouldn't assume that it's wrong; we need to stay open to the possibility that either case might turn out to be true.

Here's the key to dealing with emotions and benefitting from them rather than being overcome by them. First, we need to be aware that the unconscious mind generates emotions in response to a situation or a thought and delivers that emotion into the awareness of the conscious mind. We also need to know that we should never suppress or ignore emotions because the very fact that we have them indicates that something of importance is occurring.

But—and this is a *huge* but—we should never unconsciously react to our emotions, at least not our stronger ones.

If your boss or spouse is screaming angrily at you and you find your own anger rising, motivating you to scream (or worse) back at them, you need to learn not to suppress or ignore the emotion but to observe it and try to understand what's actually happening. You need to step out of your goldfish bowl and become objective. You need to focus on Reality A. Something really important is motivating your boss or spouse to scream at you. What is it? You need to know.

It's a time to be ruled by objectivity, not anger, because, if it's so very important to your boss or spouse, it's potentially important to you, and an angry response from you will make the situation much worse. To be sure, when you're being consciously objective, you may still *feel* angry (or fearful if that's the way you respond to anger from others), but you need your conscious mind to be in charge and objective so that you'll be able to see through your own anger (or fear) and understand the situation in order to deal with it effectively.

The very fact that emotions have arisen in ourselves or in others is both a trigger that stimulates our thoughts and behavior and an alert signaling something we need to notice. Triggers and alerts are important tools. An emotional alert is a signal telling us that something important is happening that we need to be consciously aware of and that our emotional responses should trigger us to launch into intentional and constructive behavior rather, than being reactive and destructive. I'll have more to say about triggers and alerts later.

The most concise explanation of how to deal with emotions comes from, of all places, a mystery novel by an obscure author. In *The Long Mile* by Clyde W. Ford, the author states:

> *Express. Repress. Observe. Three ways to handle emotions. It's*
> *good to express them, but not always safe. Repress them and they*
> *eat you up from inside. You can always observe them, watching*
> *what emotions do inside your body. Observe emotions and they*

> *pass through you like waves passing through water. Then you can*
> *use them as the guides they're meant to be, and not the rulers we*
> *let them become.*

The first thing to remember is that emotions, in and of themselves, never hurt anyone. They're merely feelings that come and go. Even strong emotions always fade away, leaving you with the consequences of your responses. It's our *reactions* to emotions that can lead to problems. Use emotions as "the guides they're meant to be."

The second thing about emotions is that you can't stop them, and you shouldn't try. You can repress emotions, but that's not really getting rid of them. It's just pretending they're not affecting you and behaving as if there were no emotion involved. Psychiatrists tell us that repressing emotions leads to long-term consequences like poor health, prolonged stress, and other unpleasant effects. Be that as it may, our concern is that you learn to deal with emotions in ways that support effectiveness and lead to success. And responding to emotion with emotion doesn't do that.

So you need to learn to pay attention to your emotions as if you were an uninvolved observer. Observe them, and learn how to see and hear what needs to be seen and heard through the emotion and how to behave effectively while in an emotional state.

You would think positive emotions like excitement, love, and joy would always be good, and negative emotions like fear, hate, anger, grief, and disgust would always be bad. You might not even recognize some emotions for what they are. Apathy, indifference, peace, and contentment, for instance, are low-energy emotional states, but they can exert a powerful influence on your behavior.

Depending on the situation and your response, any emotion can contribute to or detract from effectiveness and success. It all depends on the situation, your ability to recognize your own emotional state and the emotional states of those around you, and, most importantly, your ability to function effectively while awash in the presence of emotions.

The key is to use the 2Q habit to focus your mind on reality rather than letting emotion distort it. The 2Q habit doesn't eliminate your emotions, but it does force you to think rationally, even when you're flooded by emotion. It interrupts the downward spiral that emotions often take and helps you focus your attention on the situation itself rather than what it feels like, and that gets you back to a mindset that'll help you touch base with Reality A.

CHAPTER ELEVEN
Projection and the Me-Bias

Projections

We think, usually unconsciously, that the way we experience the world is the way the world actually is and that others think and perceive it the same way.

Have you ever said, "If I were in your shoes, I would…"? Did you notice that you were actually putting the other person in *your* shoes? You were projecting. You were saying what you would do in the other person's place, in effect, saying what the other person *should* do. That's what projection is all about, but it goes deeper. It's more than "should." It's a special kind of assumption that the way you view the world is the way the world is and that the way you think about things is the way everyone thinks about those things.

If you ask anyone if the way he or she thinks about things is the way everyone thinks about them, the conscious-mind answer for most of us would be an automatic "No. Not everyone thinks like I do." But your unconscious mind doesn't know this. It's another kind of WYSIATI. It knows how you think and what you think, and unless your conscious mind reins it in, it unconsciously and falsely believes that your way is *the* way that people think. Projections are almost always driven by unconscious assumptions about what's true, and of course, that truth seems true for all, or at least it does until you consciously examine it and find that there can be other ways of thinking.

I once had a conversation with a woman in which the subject of racial differences came up. Something she said made me think to myself, "What? Can she possibly believe that?" So I asked her, "Do you believe that all blacks would change to white if they could do so merely by snapping their fingers?" Her entirely sincere answer was "Yes, of course." There was no doubt, no second thought, no wondering. There was just simple certainty. To her, that's the way things are. If I had tried to talk her into a different point of view, she would have been puzzled at why I was trying to deny the truth—not the truth as she saw it but, in her mind, the plain, obvious-to-everyone truth. In those days, I didn't know what it was called, but it was my first lesson in projection.

Here's a less extreme example of two conflicting projections:

> Patricia was the owner of a small business in Northern California. She was praised by all who knew her for her ability to get results. Her friends said she was the hardest working person they knew. No matter what it took, Patricia got the job done.
>
> Sal was the general manager of Patricia's landscape supply business. Sal was a hard working guy, too, and Patricia and Sal saw eye to eye on almost everything. They enjoyed a cooperative working relationship, and Patricia almost never had to assert her authority as the boss.
>
> One day, when Sal balked at Patricia's idea of creating an emergency room for plants, they had the following conversation:

Sal: I'll do anything you want, of course, after all, it *is* your business, but this doesn't make any sense to me. It's just not worth the effort and work of creating a plant emergency room, staffing it, and publicizing it.

Patricia: But it will make us unique in our market. Effort and work don't matter. What matters is the result.

Sal: I like the result, too, but the work and hassle don't justify the result. We're already overworked and flooded with details that don't contribute much to the business. This will just make it worse.

Patricia: I don't know how to say it any more clearly. The result is the only thing that matters. The work, the details, the hassle are just what you have to do to get the job done. Sometimes, in order to get the results you want, you just have to suck it up and push through the work.

Sal: It just occurred to me that you and I see the world differently when it comes to the balance of work and results. I've always had a sense that the amount of work done should be in some reasonable proportion to the value of the results you're going for. I thought everyone saw it that way, but you don't. You really don't think about and don't even really care about what it takes to get the result you want. You just decide on the goal, the result, and push for it no matter what it takes. Is that right?

Patricia: Well, of course it's right. How could anyone ever get anything done if you worried about how hard it will be or how much work would be needed or how much hassle you'd have to put up with? I thought everyone knew that. It's just so basic, so human!

Sal: To me, it's more basic and more human to balance the goal with what it takes to make it happen. How could anybody think differently? That's just the way it is.

The discussion went on for a while, and fortunately Patricia and Sal trusted and respected each other enough to listen and really hear what the other was saying. Still, each viewpoint was so deeply and unconsciously ingrained that it was taken as a universal truth. To Patricia, it was a basic reality of the world—work and hassle are irrelevant. You don't even think about them. You do what it takes to get the job done. To Sal, it was a basic reality of the world that you always balance work and hassle against the goal. Sometimes the goal just wasn't worth it. Each of them was *projecting* an individual Reality B on the world and on each other, believing without question that it was the way of things.

That's how projection works. Your conscious and unconscious understanding of the world becomes the way the world *is*. You don't experience it as your point of view but as the fundamental truth of things.

The problem arises, of course, when you behave on the basis of your unconscious (but false) belief that it's everyone's reality and expect results consistent with that. Others are doing the same thing toward you. When someone behaves differently from your projection, you take it as a kind of violation of what's right, proper, and effective.

The way to deal with projection is to become aware that you're doing it and be alert to the possibility that others may be projecting their views on you. The two-question technique helps you do that.

The Me-Bias

I'm going to quote Kahneman again:

> *"Neither children nor adults have a well-developed capacity to distinguish the accuracy of their own beliefs. In fact, adults are particularly vulnerable with regard to maintaining self-deceptive beliefs, especially when comparing their own intelligence and at-tractiveness with other peoples'. For example, in various surveys conducted over the years, approximately 90 percent of the re-spondents believed that they were smarter, healthier, and more industrious than the average individual."*

"Most people...overestimate their personal abilities, and unfortunately their inflated beliefs cause them to suspend their ability to test reality."

We tend to be biased and self-deceiving about ourselves and, by extension, those we love and with whom we associate or feel an affinity. You know it's true of others, don't you? We all know people who exaggerate their own abilities and their own beauty and who have an inflated sense of their self worth. Why, then, isn't it obvious to us that, if others inflate their self-perceptions, we may be doing it too?

There's a self-serving logic that supports our self-deception, and it causes us to believe that we're a bit more perceptive than all those other people. Don't we know ourselves better than they do? And isn't our internal experience of ourselves the truest test of our internal reality? Of course we're the best judges of ourselves. It must be true because it *feels* so true, so certain, and if others weren't so biased toward themselves, they'd see it too.

You can see how this me-bias becomes self-fulfilling and circular in its reasoning.

There's a negative version of the me-bias in which some people come to see themselves as inferior, less worthy, or somehow not as deserving as others because of early conditioning in life. Whether positive or negative, the me-bias leads you away from the reality of yourself into self-deception.

Me-bias also extends to our perceptions of those with whom we feel some affiliation; the stronger the affiliation, the stronger the me-bias. It's usually a good thing because it makes us more cohesive and stronger as families, tribes, teams, clubs, races, religions, political parties, cultures, genders, and even whole societies.

There's a positive side to the me-bias. It may be a survival characteristic of humanity. When we see ourselves so positively, even when others don't, it makes us more willing to take on difficult tasks, assume leadership, and dream ambitious dreams.

But there's also a dark side. When me-bias becomes distorted and dysfunctional, it leads to injustice, inappropriate discrimination, and perceptions of superiority in ourselves and inferiority in others. I'd venture to say that many of humanity's man-made tragedies have their roots in me-bias. It's everywhere we look in today's society: black vs. white, Muslim vs. Christian, Republican vs. Democrat, poor vs. rich, and on and on.

The lesson for us is that me-bias is another way we distort our perceptions of reality. We don't want to eliminate me-bias because it's much too useful in our lives. But we do want to understand it and be aware of those times in our lives when it distorts our perceptions and leads us into dysfunctional behavior.

The two-question technique helps put the "me" in me-bias into the right perspective.

The Dunning-Kruger Effect: A Special Case of the Me-Bias

Did you know that *in*competent people often think they're actually very competent? Did you know that most people rate themselves much better than average, even when their actual measured performance is terrible? At some point in your life—certainly as a child—you probably felt that way.

In 1999, David Dunning and Justin Kruger explained this surprising and very fundamental aspect of the human mind in a widely respected report entitled "Unskilled and Unaware of It: How Difficulties in Recognizing One's Own Incompetence Lead to Inflated Self-Assessments."

When I first learned about Dunning-Kruger, I felt a little bit smug. I could immediately name a half dozen or so people I know who are perfect examples—they think they're highly competent in some area of expertise, but in actuality, they're not competent at all and are completely unaware of their incompetence.

Then I came down to earth. Wait a minute. Could I be guilty of this kind of thinking? If Dunning and Kruger are right (and the scientific community says they are), then we're all subject to the effect, and "all" would have to include me. So I looked at my own history, where I found some sobering examples.

I first flashed back to an important job I once had. I interviewed brilliantly and got the job, thinking to myself, "This is going to be great. Company car, bonus plan, stock options…the works." Six months later, they fired me. I wasn't competent for that job. Not only that, I didn't even know what competence for that job looked like. I do now, and I've succeeded at many jobs and major projects since those days. But at the time, I could have been the poster boy for the Dunning-Kruger effect.

Years later, it happened again, but this time I was the hiring (and firing) boss. My business coaching company needed to hire a talented writer to develop written materials for our coaches to help them teach clients how to think like entrepreneurs.

After evaluating a dozen or so candidates, we hired someone I'll call Martha, a larger-than-life woman with great credentials and an even better persona. She was charismatic, assertive, and confident. We *knew* she was right for the job…but she wasn't. She bombed. Not only could she not write the materials we needed, but she also couldn't even understand what was needed even though we showed her dozens of examples that we had already created and which were being used successfully with our clients out there in the real world.

I clearly remember firing her because it got loud. She said that it was *our* incompetence that was the problem. We weren't qualified to judge her, and she was the best writer we had ever met. And if it wasn't that, then we were prejudiced against women. That one didn't fly because a woman helped me hire Martha, and she was, by the way, an excellent writer of exactly the kind of materials that we needed. She urged me to fire Martha even before I had reached that conclusion myself.

When it became clear to Martha that she wasn't going to cure my talent blindness or stupidity, she stood up, used a few choice phrases (involving my ancestry and a difficult to accomplish sexual practice), and stomped out, never to be seen again. I recall a slammed door.

To be fair, most of us are competent about many things: our jobs, our education, and our special interests, all of which we spend time and effort on to develop extensive knowledge and expertise. We actually are competent about these things, and our confidence is justified. But for the really complicated things we encounter in life—politics, the economy, global warming, religion, the stock market, the prison/corrections system, marital relationships, medical problems, philosophy, race relations, or even sports—our knowledge, experience, and reasoning are limited. For those areas, we're incompetent. But we don't always know it.

Dunning and Kruger say that lacking understanding of a subject means that we also lack the ability to make accurate judgments about our skill in that area. They say that knowing a little bit makes us feel smart about that little bit, and we think we've got it covered. When we fail, we attribute our failure to other factors such as prejudices, other people's incompetence, circumstances beyond our control—anything but our own incompetence. And we maintain the illusion of competence even when our lack of competence is obvious to others.

We can dodge the Dunning-Kruger effect if we have a little bit of self-awareness and a lot of humility. I'm constantly asking myself when I might be in over my head, "Do I really know as much as I think I do?" or "Am I as good as I think I am?"

The 2Q habit is especially helpful. By turning the two questions on ourselves and looking at ourselves from the point of view of an uninvolved observer, we can discover a lot of truths about ourselves. What's reality (about me)? What are the possibilities (for me)? The 2Q habit helps us see beyond our goldfish bowls so we can make the appropriate adjustments.

CHAPTER TWELVE
Focus Blindness and Stress

Your unconscious mind has a mind of its own, and it doesn't always see what's there to be seen.

Have you ever been so absorbed with a task or experience that you didn't hear someone say something to you? Or maybe you did hear the sound but had to have it repeated so you could truly hear it? "I'm sorry, I didn't hear what you said. Would you please repeat it?"

Have you ever been playing a game or working so intently that you injured yourself, yet you didn't feel any pain until later? Soldiers in battle sometimes get wounded yet feel no pain, and sometimes they don't even know they're wounded until later when they discover, usually with considerable surprise, that they've been wounded. Athletes often get minor injuries without being aware of them until later when the intensity of the competition abates and the intensity of the injury becomes noticeable.

When you focus your attention on something, you become less aware of other things, sometimes even blind to them. The more intently you focus, the more blind you become to everything else. And when you're blind, your Reality B won't match up with Reality A.

There is a famous experiment that illustrates the effect. You can see it on the Internet. Go to YouTube and look for "The Monkey Business Illusion." Follow the instructions carefully, and you'll be surprised at your own powers of observation—or lack thereof. Don't read the next paragraph until after you've watched the Monkey Business Illusion. It's worth the experience. Take a break from reading, and go check out some Monkey Business.

* * *

Those of you who watched the Monkey Business Illusion experienced focus blindness in dramatic, if humorous, fashion. For those of you who didn't bother to watch, the Monkey Business Illusion consists of six people, three in black shirts and three in white shirts, moving around in a room, passing basketballs back and forth between themselves. As an observer, your task is to count the number of times people in white shirts pass the ball to other people in white shirts, ignoring the times that people in black shirts pass or receive. It becomes a confusing scene, and it requires concentration and focus to get an accurate count.

But the point of the exercise isn't to count basketball passes. It's to demonstrate focus blindness. What happens is that, after about thirty seconds of watching, counting, and focusing your attention on the exercise, a person in a gorilla suit walks slowly among the basketball passers, pauses in the middle of the room to beat its chest, and then walks out of the room.

Most people don't even notice the gorilla, and they have to watch the video again to convince themselves that there actually was a gorilla and that they missed it completely. Even people like me who think we're savvy and who know about the Monkey Business Illusion fall prey to focus blindness. I know about the Monkey Business Illusion, but during the exercise, the color of the background curtain changes, and one of the six people leaves the room, and I didn't notice anything but the basketballs and the gorilla. So even though I was prepared to have my powers of observation tested, I was still blind to two significant happenings in the exercise. It's mind-blowing.

What happens is that, when confronted with a task that requires focused attention, your mind channels itself to accomplish the task. Your eyes, ears, etc. continue to receive sensory data, but your mind is ignoring everything not related to the task on which you're focused. Your eyes see the gorilla and pass on that visual data, but your mind doesn't pay attention to it because it has nothing to do with the task of counting basketball passes. The resources of the mind are dedicated to accomplishing the task, and it ignores what it considers irrelevant.

Expectations also have something to do with it. If you were told beforehand that a gorilla would appear, you'd have noticed the gorilla even though you were concentrating on basketball passing. Training and awareness can open your powers of observation so that you're less susceptible to focus blindness, but even the best training can't overcome the mind's need to narrow its perceptions to the task at hand, especially when the task is important and difficult.

Stress is a bit different, but it can also diminish your powers of observation and mess with your thinking. Stress occurs when you're experiencing some form of real or imagined threat. It could be a real danger, the possibility of failure in an important endeavor, a real or imagined embarrassment or possibility of suffering a blow to your self-image, or anything else that produces stress in you. When stressed, your mind becomes preoccupied with the real or imagined situation that's stressing you, and you aren't as alert to the world as you would normally be. You might fail to notice things you would normally notice. You tend to make decisions more erratically. You don't think as quickly as you normally would. You tend to make more mistakes. You get overwhelmed more easily. You can more easily misinterpret or overreact to the words and acts of others.

In either case, whether focus or stress, your mind ignores some perceptions and/or reshapes some perceptions to be consistent with the real or imagined situation. The result is that your mental model (your Reality B) gets distorted, and you're not dealing with reality but with a flawed perception of reality. And that means decisions and actions that you take when intently focused or stressed may not be completely based in reality.

What's the conclusion? When you're stressed or highly focused, you're not as rational as you think you are. Not completely. The greater the stress and the more intense the focus, the less rational you are. Yet the mind, especially the unconscious mind (because it automatically seeks and often creates coherency) believes its decisions and actions to be completely rational and justifiable.

In this case, the 2Q habit doesn't open you up to information and possibilities as much as it awakens you to what's right in front of you. It activates your awareness so that you're more likely to see what's there to be seen, heard, felt, etc.

CHAPTER THIRTEEN

Jumping To Conclusions

We all jump to conclusions. We can't help it. We're wired that way, and it's a good thing…most of the time. But when it's not, it can lead to all kinds of mischief and conflict.

Why do we jump to conclusions? Our brains evolved at a time when the world was more primitive, and jumping to conclusions could save your life. A swaying patch of grass might be just the wind, or it could be a deadly saber-toothed tiger. If our ancestors paused to think about the situation, the result could have been fatal, but if they drew the quick conclusion—Tiger!—and ran away, well, no harm done.

Today's world is a much more complex place, much of it beyond our understanding, and very little of it life threatening, but the evolution of our brains hasn't kept up with the evolution of the world around us, so we still jump to conclusions.

To explain it, let me call yet again on my favorite expert of the mind, Daniel Kahneman. He's the one who explained that the unconscious mind bases all its thinking on whatever information, experience, and unconscious mental habits we have accumulated over the years—remember WYSIATI?—because, to the unconscious mind, "what you see is all there is." Kahneman tells us that the unconscious mind assumes that everything it knows is complete (even when it isn't), assumes it's true (even when it isn't), and uses that knowledge to come up with ideas and opinions, which it delivers to our conscious minds with great certainty. And because it's an *unconscious* process, we're not even aware that it's happening. We just suddenly think we know what's true.

Kahneman also tells us that the unconscious mind doesn't doubt itself. That's the job of the conscious mind. So conclusions that bubble up from the unconscious mind seem highly certain unless we double-check them with our conscious judgment, which we don't normally do but can learn to do.

I don't know about you, but personally, I don't want to jump to a conclusion if it's wrong because wrong opinions often lead to stupid decisions, and basically, I don't want to be stupid. So how can I avoid this kind of stupidity?

It all comes back to WYSIATI and the knowledge (or lack of it) contained in our unconscious minds. WYSIATI causes us to jump to conclusions based on limited and often insufficient evidence. It causes us to have unwarranted confidence in our conclusions. The confidence that individuals have in their beliefs depends mostly on the quality of the story they can tell about what they see, even if they see little. Have you ever noticed that people who only see one-sided evidence are more confident of their judgments than those who see both sides?

People with extensive education, training, and experience have filled their unconscious minds with more and better knowledge, so their WYSIATIs are packed with more complete and more reliable information. As a result, they jump to more reliable, reality-based conclusions.

It's really pretty simple. The more we know about something, the better our conclusions about it; the less we know, the more likely we are to be wrong, no matter how confident we feel.

So what's the bottom line here? How can we avoid jumping to false conclusions?

First and foremost, we need to be constantly aware that our minds are designed to jump to conclusions no matter how much or how little we know and that they're also designed so that we'll feel confident about our opinions, even when confidence isn't justified. Then we need to question ourselves. The 2Q habit is perfect for this. Do we really know as much as we think we do? Are our opinions based in reality and factual? Are they as solid as they feel? Are there other ways to see the situation?

It's up to us to use our conscious minds to reality check ourselves and question those conclusions we jump to so easily.

Three Steps to Stupid

When we go stupid, it seems to happen as a three-step process, and it involves several of our cognitive habits. It starts when we jump to conclusions and emotionally feel good about those conclusions. Our conclusions may be right or wrong, but they seem right to us—they *feel* right, intuitively and emotionally—so we don't question them. Then the confirmation bias takes charge and we prove to ourselves that our conclusions were right and that our version of reality is *the* reality. Sometimes we get it right, sometimes we don't. And when we don't, we think, believe, say, or do stupid things.

It's an unconscious process—three steps to stupid—and it goes like this:

Step One: Jumping to Conclusions. When you first see someone, experience a situation, hear a new idea, or have a thought about something, your unconscious mind makes all kinds of associations and connections and tries to make sense of it. Your mind is really good at this, and it always provides you with some kind of initial impression—you jump to a conclusion, however accurate or inaccurate that conclusion may be.

Step Two: Emotional and Intuitive Reinforcement. Because your initial impression fits with what you already know (or think you know), you feel pretty sure about it. If you're not aware that first impressions can lead you astray, it feels right. You're not certain yet, but your mind is biased to reinforce your first impression, and it's a little bit resistant to other possibilities. Steps one and two happen almost simultaneously; your mind jumps to a conclusion, and it feels right.

Step Three: Confirmation Bias. At the unconscious level, the human mind tends to reinforce our initial impressions and ignore other possibilities. So we confirm what we think we already know, we selectively pay attention to information that is consistent with that, and we selectively ignore or downplay information that isn't. In short, we tend to confirm our first impressions and downplay other possibilities even when our first impressions turn out to be wrong.

Here's a little scenario that shows how it works.

Sal meets Wayne. She feels uneasy about Wayne, but she doesn't know why. Unknown to Sal, her unconscious mind has made the association that Wayne's eyes look a lot like the eyes of a serial killer she saw in a television documentary, and he has a similar kind of nervous energy. Except for the uneasy feeling, none of this registers in Sal's conscious mind, but she is instantly biased to dislike or maybe even fear Wayne because of these unconscious associations.

Very quickly, her mind reinforces her uneasiness because his gravelly voice, big strong hands, and height all seem threatening. Normally, Sal would be attracted to a gravelly voice and big hands on a tall man, but her unconscious mind had already biased her perceptions negatively. She was primed to see things in a threatening way, and, of course, when she did, those details confirmed her initial uneasiness and increased it. At a conscious level, all of this made her think, "There's something creepy about Wayne. He gives off a threatening vibe."

Of course, Wayne gave off no such vibe. It was all generated by Sal's unconscious mental associations. Unless Sal is given a reason to reconsider her impressions of Wayne, she'll continue to see things about him that will confirm her first impression.

It could have gone the other way. If Sal had unconsciously reacted to Wayne's athletic posture and good looks, which her unconscious mind associates with desirable men, those big hands and gravelly voice might have seemed attractive rather than creepy. All that would have biased her first impressions favorably, and she would have been primed to notice more good things about Wayne than bad. She might even have been attracted to him.

All this is greatly simplified, of course. The human mind, conscious and unconscious, is amazingly complex. But the underlying dynamic—experience a first impression, have positive or negative feelings about it, and thereafter be biased to confirm the first impression—works in all of us.

How can we know if our conclusions are valid or not? We can introduce a fourth step into our thinking—a conscious step. We can deliberately take notice of our own reactions. We can withhold our initial judgment and expand our awareness to take in the full spectrum of initial impressions: positive, negative, and neutral.

The 2Q habit helps us do this. Sal can dislike Wayne's eyes and other negative impressions about him, but she can also consciously withhold her negative judgment and ask herself the two questions. She can see more, hear more, allow more unconscious associations to connect, and form a more balanced first impression. If Sal learns to do that, she'll have a more accurate understanding of the truth about Wayne and also about other people, things, and ideas.

And if Sal can learn to avoid the three steps to stupid, so can we.

CHAPTER FOURTEEN

The Duality of Experience

Experience as History:
The Way Things Were Isn't Necessarily the Way Things Are

You've probably heard this before: "We've always done it this way, and it's always been successful, so we're going to do it this way again." Sooner or later, "We've always done it this way" will become a formula for failure.

Ask Kmart if "we've always done it this way" is a valid way to manage a business. In 1986, Kmart was at the top of the heap in its industry. Management was complacent and persisted with the same strategy that had been so successful in the past. Meanwhile, Walmart and Target were creating new ways of doing things and siphoning off Kmart's customers. When Kmart finally woke up, it was too late. In 2004, Walmart had become the largest retailer in the world. Kmart was bankrupt and shedding stores in a panic to survive. Walmart changed. Kmart didn't.

Experience is a great teacher, maybe the greatest. But times and situations change, making old ways of doing things obsolete. And the changes often happen slowly, so the old way of doing things slowly becomes less and less effective as it becomes more and more out of tune with changing times.

Or maybe not. Sometimes the tried and true way of doing things is still best.

The point is this: of course we should learn from experience and respect what has worked for us in the past...but not blindly. We must be open to and willing to adapt to changes. Better yet, we should anticipate changes and take advantage of them rather than being victimized by them. And still better, we should be willing to *initiate* changes that will enable us to achieve our goals.

Internal Experience:
It Makes Life Worth Living, But Sometimes It Lies

I have a very good friend. When I think she's imagining things, she tells me that she trusts her experience and that her experience *is* her reality. She's both right and wrong, but it took me a lot of years to understand why.

Let's look at Reality A and Reality B from a different point of view and talk about Reality B as your internal experience. Let's start with something that doesn't carry much emotional load. Let's talk about rainbows.

Rainbows don't actually exist. They're a creation of our minds in response to physical signals processed by our brains. The factuality of a rainbow is that it's a phenomenon in which electromagnetic waves (light) pass through droplets of water in the atmosphere, with waves of different frequencies being bent at slightly different angles. That's the short version of Reality A; the bent electromagnetic waves are detected by our eyes, and our eyes pass signals into our brains. Our brains interpret these signals as colors.

Reality A: Electromagnetic waves in the frequency range of 400-484 terahertz.

Reality B: Red.

There's something objectively real in the world that we perceive when we see rainbows. The world creates a phenomenon following the laws of physics and produces objective results in the form of bent rays of light. Our minds perceive that phenomenon and create internal experiences shaped by our senses, our brains' bioelectrochemical activity, habits of thinking, habits of being, and mental models. The resulting experience is a rainbow.

That's our Reality B despite the fact that we can't touch a rainbow. We can't even get near one. As we get closer, it either seems to move farther away or disappears. No one has ever touched a rainbow or even found the foot of one, where leprechauns supposedly hide their pots of gold.

Which is true, the objective reality or the internal experience? Reality A or Reality B?

They're both true—they both exist, one as objective reality and the other as our internal experience.

And here's the wonderful thing about rainbows: they're beautiful. Do you know anyone who doesn't think so? The beauty of a rainbow lies in our internal experience, not in its factuality. In fact, beauty itself exists only within us. The external world is what it is; the perception of beauty (the experience) exists only within us, and it's probably different for each of us.

External reality may trigger our experiences, but it's the internal experience that gives the phenomenon value, stimulates our emotions, and makes us feel alive.

Let's move away from rainbows. What about love? Does love exist in the external world? I say no. Love exists in our internal experiences. To the extent that we can act lovingly and communicate our internal experiences with each other, we can share love, but there's nothing outside of us that we can point to as the external reality of love—no electromagnetic waves passing through droplets and no other physical phenomenon.

Yet love is among our most powerful experiences and one of our strongest motivators. So are hate, fear, anger, and joy. None of our emotions exist in the external world; they're all created by us as part of our internal experience.

Here's the problem: our internal experience is triggered by external realities or the perception of external realities, but we don't always perceive external realities as they actually are but rather as our internal experience tells us they are. That's okay when we're looking at rainbows and experiencing the beauty and wonder of them. It's not okay when we make life-changing decisions, manage our relationships, spend our money, start businesses, lead others into war, pass laws, make judgments in court, or try to manage our health based on perceptions of reality and internal experiences that are not consistent with the factuality of Reality A.

Con men, sales people, politicians, advertisers, advocates for all kinds of causes, and all manner of others depend on our human tendency to respond to our internal experiences as if they accurately reflected the external reality. They spend a lot of time, thought, and effort to help you construct a favorable experience of them and getting you to trust them so that they can have their way with you. Often, their way isn't what you expected or wanted and isn't at all in your best interests. It's in cases like these that you need to be aware that your internal experience isn't necessarily reality, even if it seems to be and even if you want it to be. Important decisions that affect your quality of life and well-being must be Reality A-based, or they'll be, at best, disappointing and, at worst, life-threatening or costly in other ways.

So it's critically important to be able to make distinctions between Reality A and our internal experiences. We don't want to eliminate our internal experiences, not even the ones that aren't fact based; they make us human and provide much of what's valuable and beautiful in life. That's an important reason for eliminating cognitive biases—they distort our perceptions, and that results in distorted Reality Bs. But important decisions and plans absolutely *must* be Reality A-based regardless of whether our internal experiences are inconsistent or contradictory.

But how? When a flawed Reality B *feels* real and we unconsciously cling to the false reality of it, how can we anchor ourselves in Reality A without losing the value and wonder of our internal experience?

Well, as long as you can distinguish between Reality A and your internal experience (Reality B), then no harm, no foul. For instance, can't you know that rainbows are in actuality nothing more than bent electromagnetic energy yet still hold and enjoy the experience of their beauty? Sure you can, and you should. Can't you know that the experience of love is created within you and your loved ones and has no external reality yet still deeply love those near and dear to you and be loved by them? Sure you can, and you should.

What happens when your Reality B overwhelms your decisions? For instance, don't most of us marry for love rather than some objective analytical reason? Love is one of those emotions that distorts our thinking, isn't it? Again, you need to be aware of the Reality A of your beloved and then consciously choose to override Reality A in favor of the love that shapes your Reality B. If you love a scoundrel, and know he is a scoundrel yet still want to marry, it's a very bad idea, but at least you'll know what you're getting into. I advise against marrying scoundrels, but if that's your choice, go into it with eyes wide open so you can deal with the consequences that are likely to challenge your marriage, maybe doom it.

When the stakes are high, and you're making life-altering decisions, you'd better get your Reality B in tune with Reality A, or there'll be trouble.

The 2Q habit gets you there.

PERSONALITY HABITS
(HABITS OF BEING)

CHAPTER FIFTEEN

Personality Habits (Habits of Being)

How Your Personality Might Be Getting in Your Way

Personality habits seem to be more deeply anchored in your unconscious self than cognitive habits. They can be more difficult to discover, more subtle in their operation, and more difficult to shift. The interplay of habits of thinking with the more deeply anchored personality habits reflects the interplay and interconnectedness of the brain itself. It all works together seamlessly, and the distinction between thinking and being is actually artificial. They both arise from the same source, and like your arms and legs, they're different, but they're all parts of the same body, and they collectively cause you to function the way you do.

These next few chapters will help you answer three questions:

- What are personality habits, and where do they come from?

- Which of your personality habits are distorting your thinking and your behavior?

- What can you do about them?

I admit, I'm nervous about these next few chapters. My fear for you in these chapters is that you won't like them. I'm afraid that you'll skim them, not like what you see, and skip them. Or maybe you'll actually read them carefully, think "Got it," and go on without engaging in the internal discovery they ask of you. If you do that, if you're intimidated by the work required, impatient, or simply don't see the benefit in this particular form of self-discovery, you'll miss out on some of the most valuable insights people can learn about themselves. Your most deeply hidden blockages will remain deeply hidden and therefore unknown to you. They'll sabotage you when you most need to succeed, and you won't know why it's happening. You'll blame others, circumstances, or even yourself, all the while being puzzled about what did or didn't happen. And your pattern will repeat, cause unknown, into the future.

So my request is that you take these chapters seriously. They're worth your time and effort, so commit to them. Be open to their possibilities. Give them your best effort and see what comes out the other end. I predict that you'll be glad you did.

What Are Personality Habits, and Where Do They Come From?

Do you know someone who is shy, intelligent, kind, and generous? Do you know someone who is aggressive, mean-spirited, and argumentative? Do you know someone who is bland, boring, and a loner? All those characteristics and many more are personality traits—habitual ways of being and behaving—and they make each of us a distinct and unique individual. Optimism is a personality habit, and so is pessimism. And so are procrastination, perfectionism, bullying, conflict avoidance, skepticism, compassion, competitiveness, a sense of responsibility, ambition, honesty, dishonesty, and a limitless number of others, all of them running unconsciously in our heads and making us who we are and all of them contributing to or blocking our success.

Personality habits are important because not only do they influence your Reality B, but they also influence the ways you interact with others, how you make decisions, and the manner in which you behave and take action. If you're going to be an effective and impactful person, your habits of being need to be appropriate to the situations you encounter.

These deep-seated drivers of our thoughts and behavior seem to be partly genetic but mostly learned. Either way, they show up in our earliest days. It all happens without our knowing it, and these habits persist throughout our lives unless we become aware of them and choose to do something about them.

Let me show you how habits of being typically develop using the example of a brother and sister. The brother and sister are real, but I'll respect their privacy and call them Jerry and Susan.

Jerry and Susan's father was a complex man. He was angry much of the time, but he had a soft spot for the helpless and for the underdog. When Jerry was a tiny child, probably around the time he was potty-trained and certainly earlier than he can remember, he found that he couldn't resist or rebel against his father under any circumstances. If he did, it aroused his father's instant anger and often earned Jerry a spanking. Jerry was afraid of his father; he loved him but was deeply fearful of his anger and would go to great lengths not to provoke it.

So Jerry unconsciously learned that he could prevent the threat of a spanking and reduce his fear by avoiding and withdrawing, all without thinking about it. How could he? He was less than two years old. He never opposed his father, and when his dad's anger threatened, Jerry held his tongue and withdrew. Later, he found that he didn't have to physically withdraw or avoid his father; he could withdraw and avoid internally. It became his pattern of be-havior with his father. And later, it became his pattern of behavior with any strong personality in his life. And even later, it became his pattern of behavior in any situation where real or imagined conflict and anger might occur. And now, it's his innate habit of conflict avoidance, and it's often a counterproductive one. When the situation calls for Jerry to stand his ground and engage with other people to get something done, Jerry avoids and withdraws.

And he does it automatically, habitually, with no awareness that he's doing it.

The early childhood pattern became the unconscious way that Jerry dealt with what he perceived as strong personalities and situations, real or imagined, that held the threat of conflict. The pattern shifted over the years and became an adult version, but it remained his habitual way of dealing with things. It's more complex than that, of course, and there are many other drivers of Jerry's personality, some of which are quite effective. For instance, he's patient, understanding, readily sees other people's points of view, and has a first-rate mind for strategy, among many other virtues. But in times of stress, he's predominantly driven by avoidance and withdrawal, and he's not even aware of it. It's just the way he is.

The point is that Jerry's patterns took shape in his very early life, became unconscious behaviors of mind and action, shifted a little in response to his later experiences, but basically stayed the same and had a lot to do with shaping him as a person. The little boy who avoided and withdrew from his father's anger is still the internal little boy who drives Jerry's life now.

Jerry's sister, Susan, had the same father and lived in the same environment, but she developed differently. Dad had a soft spot for little girls, and Susan quickly learned a successful way of coping at such a young age that she has no memory of it. Instead of withdrawing, she turned on the charm and became helpful to her father in any way she could. That completely disarmed him and turned off his anger. She derived a sense of power and control from it. She never developed a fear-based response. She learned that she could manage her circumstances by appealing to her father through charm and helpfulness.

That pattern persisted, and today's adult version of it has Susan developing cooperative relationships, networking, and helping other people succeed. It's more complex than that for Susan, too, and she has some ineffective habits of being. For instance, she's a bit narcissistic, she jumps to unwarranted assumptions quickly, and she tends to take the easy way when a more difficult path might yield better results. But the little girl who charmed and helped her way into her father's good graces is still the internal little girl who drives her life now.

Every one of us has our own versions of Jerry's and Susan's early years and a comparable development of our own habits of being. The key points to keep in mind are these:

Much of our thinking and behavior are driven by deeply held, mostly unconscious patterns of thought and behavior that had their origins in our earliest years. Depending on our circumstances, these patterns (our personality habits) either help or hinder us in our quest for success.

To increase our effectiveness in life, we must identify the personality habits that inhibit us and convert them into more effective habits.

Personality Habits Are Often Obvious to Others But Invisible to Ourselves

Personality habits are deeply ingrained, and we don't pay much attention to them because they're automatic, they operate unconsciously, and they seem normal and right. They're like our bones; we can't see them, and we don't notice them, but they shape us and everything we do, and they also limit everything we do. We know about our bones, but we don't pay them much attention. We can pay attention to them any time we want, but if they're not broken or diseased, why would we? We just let them do what they do and go on about our lives.

Personality habits are a lot like that. If you habitually avoid conflict, as Jerry does, you don't pay much attention to that habit. It's just the way you are, and that's how you do things. Most likely, you're not even aware of it. If things occasionally don't work out the way you expect, you wouldn't make the connection between the event and your personality; it's *that* invisible, especially in the moment it's happening. If Jerry's conflict avoidance is brought to his attention, his unconscious mind will respond to his me-bias and reframe it, and he'll see himself as diplomatic and agreeable, not as a conflict avoider.

For a contrasting example, take someone who is aggressive and impulsive. If it's brought to her attention that she's aggressive and impulsive, her unconscious mind reframes that idea and convinces her that she's assertive, not aggressive, and decisive rather than impulsive, and that's just fine; it's just the way she is. She may see the habit as a weakness or a strength, but it's okay, or it's no big deal, and anyway, it's just the way she is. And again, most likely, she's not even aware of its impact on others. When things occasionally don't work out for her, she wouldn't normally make the connection between the event and being aggressive and impulsive or, in Jerry's case, conflict avoidant.

We *need* to become aware, and we *need* to make the connections between our personality habits and the events in our lives when they're not working out as we want and expect them to. If we want to be more successful human beings, we need to be aware when our habits of being are blocking us, and we need to do something about them. So the first task is awareness; we need to identify the habits of being that are blocking us—let's call them *blocker habits*.

Identifying blocker habits is easier said than done. If all these habits are unconscious and automatic and therefore invisible to us as we live our lives (and make our mistakes), just how do we become aware of them? We do it by looking at our own history and focusing on our unsuccessful experiences. We do it by identifying those disappointing situations we have personally experienced and drilling down to find out what it was about ourselves that blocked us from making the most of each situation.

When confronted with our failures, most of us come up with all kinds of reasons for failing. We rationalize, and we don't even know we're doing it. Those reasons are nothing but excuses. They bubble up from the unconscious mind, which doesn't want us to think of ourselves as anything less than great, or the self-negating attitude that doesn't want us to think we're great. It's a blaming mentality that wants all the problems in life to be caused by some external force; It does anything to avoid having to admit that "I failed" and will find a way to lay the cause of failure at some other doorstep.

So accept it. Whatever disappointment we've experienced and whatever failure has happened on our watch, it's on us. That's the beginning of the personal discovery process—deciding to learn what it was *about ourselves* that resulted in disappointing results and unanticipated consequences.

Why Would We Want to Change?

Converting our personality habits can feel like changing our personalities because that's exactly what it is. Most of us don't want to do that. To our unconscious minds, different equals bad and similar equals good. So if I ask you to change some of your personality habits, your unconscious mind thinks I'm asking you to become, first of all, something you're not, and secondly, something bad, undesirable, or less than you are now.

Why would an aggressive person want to become weaker? Why would an optimist want to become negative? Why would a compassionate person want to become hard-hearted? Why would a considerate, peaceful person want to generate conflict and opposition? Why would a skeptic want to become gullible? Why would a competitive person want to become a loser? And on and on.

For each habit in our personalities, there is an alternative way of being, and the alternatives seem foreign to us...they just don't feel right. We don't want to be some other way because our way feels better, normal, and right. But is it?

I'm not going to insist that you change. I don't have the power or the inclination to do that anyway; it's not my right. But if you're willing, I am going to help you discover for yourself the personality habits that aren't working for you, give you a way to convert them into habits of your own design that *will* work for you, and leave the choice up to you. You will decide whether or not to commit to a change. And then you will make the change...or not. It's all up to you.

Returning to the questions above: Why would an aggressive person want to become weaker? He wouldn't. But he would want to become smarter and more creative, and channel his aggressiveness into productive actions when the situation calls for it. Why would an optimist want to become negative? She wouldn't. But she would want to understand the difference between optimism and realism when the situation calls for it. Why would a compassionate person want to become hard-hearted? He wouldn't. But he would want to apply his compassion appropriately, for instance, when making a decision that might bring harm or discomfort to a few, but which would bring greater benefit to a much larger population. Why would a competitive person want to become a loser? She wouldn't. But she would want to accept a lesser short-term result in favor of a better (and winning) long-term result. These are examples of looking at situations and yourself from a different point of view, and also of being objective so that you can determine if Reality A about yourself is different from what you think it is, and so you can learn if there are some aspects of your personality that may be holding you back, getting in your way, and diminishing your effectiveness...in other words, blocking you.

The only one who can make valid judgments about you is you. But if you're like most of us, you'll need a little help.

The starting point is self-discovery.

CHAPTER SIXTEEN

Are Your Personality Habits Blocking You? A Process for Self-Discovery

A Very Personal Story

When I was well into middle age, I learned for the first time that something about my personality was blocking me. At the time, I was working for a husband and wife team who owned and managed a small business. I reported to both of them separately, and I had different responsibilities to each. One morning, at the beginning of the workday, I was called into the conference room. It was a door closed meeting, so I knew there was trouble. They didn't beat around the bush. "Alex, you have been playing us off against each other. You know we disagree about our business strategy, but you support each of us against the other. It's dishonest at a minimum and certainly disloyal to the company. Tell us why we shouldn't fire you immediately."

I was aghast. They were right, and I hadn't even realized I was doing it.

Here's what was happening: I would listen to him, hear his thoughts about strategy for the business, and then give him the reasons for favoring that strategy without mentioning the reasons against. I gave him the pros but not the cons. I did the same thing with her. I gave each of them half of my thinking...the half that supported his/her ideas but not the half that didn't. I was avoiding the debate and potential arguments. I didn't want to take sides or get stuck in the middle of their battle. I imagined that I would be trapped between them if I gave them honest, complete pro *and* con feedback, which, of course, was what they both wanted and needed.

I told them my side of the story, which saved my job but left them with a lot of doubt about me, doubt that tainted their trust for more than a year.

In my mind, I was being supportive to each of them for the strategies they wanted to employ in their business. What they needed from me was truthful and intelligent feedback. What they got from me was support for their individual but conflicting strategies. I was actually adding to their conflict rather than helping them move beyond it. I had the knowledge and background to help them forge an effective strategy—that's why they hired me in the first place—but I was blocked by a personality habit I didn't even know I had. I was a conflict avoider, but at that time, I didn't realize it. To them, I looked like a sycophantic weasel, seeking their approval in a two-faced way, saying what each one wanted to hear.

In later years, as I learned more about how the unconscious mind works, I slowly came to understand what it means to be a conflict avoider. In the case of the husband and wife team, I was avoiding both real and imaginary conflict, and in doing so, I missed a major opportunity to help them find the best aspects of their thinking so that they could craft a new strategy, one that would take full advantage of their thinking—and mine—and lead all of us to the best chance for success.

I also came to understand that throughout my adolescent and adult life up to that point, I had been doing the same thing: avoiding real or imagined conflict. And I was completely unaware that I was doing it. Many times in my early career, I sabotaged myself with this same behavior. I remember one time a coworker I respected and trusted said to me, "Alex, I don't know what you stand for. Sometimes you need to stand up and be counted." She was right because I seemed either to agree with everything or to hold back with no opinions about anything. Either I was avoiding the potential of getting caught up in conflict and disagreeing about a proposal, or I wouldn't make any proposals myself for fear of disagreement.

It took a process similar to the one laid out in this chapter for me to understand what was happening and how my unconscious mind had been conditioned long ago, to avoid confrontation, conflict, and the strong negative emotions associated with those situations. I still have the instincts of a conflict avoider, but now, at long last, I recognize when it's happening so that I can choose my behavior—avoid conflict when cooperation and support will be more effective or stand up and be counted when that is appropriate to the situation.

We often have counterproductive personality traits that are completely hidden from our awareness. They can be useful, productive traits in some situations yet counterproductive in others. They can, and often do, block us from progress, from growth, from fully satisfying relationships, and from having the kinds of lives we want.

It's a good bet that you have one or more personality traits that can, in some situations, block you from being your best self. It's also a good bet that you're unaware of them. If you're like the majority of us, you're reframing these traits in your mind as good, useful behavior, just as I did when thinking of myself as diplomatic and agreeable. Your blocker habits are almost certain to be different from mine, but it's another good bet that you have at least one or, more probably, a few of them.

This chapter is all about identifying the personality habits that block us. The next chapter will tell us what we can do about them.

The Discovery Process: What Are *Your* Blockers?

I cobbled together this discovery process from a combination of sources, notably:

- Daniel Kahneman's book, *Thinking Fast and Slow)*, which I've already cited several times.

- Michael Ray's book *The Highest Goal.* Michael also gave me personal guidance when I was teaching my favorite course, *Leadership, Ethics, and Creativity in business.* Michael was highly respected for his decades of research and his popular course on business creativity at Stanford University.

- My own decades of research and development while coaching would-be entrepreneurs and helping them become aware of their counter-productive habits and guiding their conversion toward more effective habits.

First, let me give you an overview of the process so you'll know where we're headed. The process is a bit complicated, and it requires a lot of introspection of the sort we wouldn't normally do, but that's what it takes to penetrate our own self-justifications (remember the me-bias?) so that we can uncover those aspects of our personalities that lie hidden in our unconscious minds.

Overview of the Blocker Discovery Process

1. Create a **bad news list** containing the experiences in your life that were significant disappointments or outright failures.

2. Select an experience from your bad news list and mentally relive that experience, using something called the **eight-sense experience technique**.

3. Create a **diagnostic ladder** showing the reasons the experience was not as successful as you intended or expected it to be.

4. Probe each of those reasons to discover your blockers, using the **repeating question technique**. Probe deeply in order to go beyond your cognitive biases and to discover if a blocker contributed to your disappointment.

5.   Look for your patterns and priorities, and write the answer to this question: "What personality habits got in my way, and how did they interfere with my success?"

6.   Select another experience from your bad news list, and do steps 2–5 again. Continue to do this until the results become repetitious and you have revealed which cognitive biases and personality traits habitually block you and under what circumstances they block you.

7.   Create a prioritized list of personality traits that tend to block you— your **blocker list**—containing the cognitive biases and personality habits that tend to diminish your thinking and behavior.

As you search for your blockers, you'll notice that habits of *thinking*—cognitive biases—will show up as well. In fact, you'll probably identify your cognitive biases first because they're less deeply anchored in your unconscious mind, less hidden from your awareness, and you've already put significant time and attention to learning about them and how they operate within you.

Don't stop the discovery process when you uncover cognitive biases, but stick with it and go deeper until you've discovered any and all personality habits that are blocking you. You'll see how to do this as you read through the details of the discovery process. I'll walk you through those details one step at a time.

Step 1: Create a bad news list containing the experiences in your life that were significant disappointments or outright failures.

What's the starting point for unearthing the habits of being that block you?

The starting point is you. Your life. Your experiences. The parts of your personal history when things went wrong or when they turned out in unexpected, unwelcome ways. It's the failures, disappointments, misfortunes, wrong expectations, and big bets that didn't work out that hold the secrets to what's blocking you.

The first step is to make a list of things that went wrong or fell short of your expectations over the course of your life—call it your bad news list.

The experiences you identify could be outright failures, achievements that fell short of your goals, important predictions or expectations that didn't pan out as you thought they would, or any other situations that didn't turn out for you or that you dealt with poorly.

By the way, forces of nature, diseases, acts of God, and other uncontrollable situations should be included in your list because even though they were beyond your control, you still had to deal with them when they occurred. Clear, unbiased thinking, unblocked by flawed habits of mind, would have enabled you to deal with your bad news experiences more successfully than you did when they happened. You might have minimized the damage and sometimes even thrived in the face of the adversity.

So take a few minutes to write down a list of the times, experiences, events in your life that didn't turn out as you wanted or expected them to. Include all of your disappointments, big and small—your failures, departures from what you expected, goals that you didn't reach, and goals you reached that turned out not to have been the right ones. List all the negative experiences in your life in which you played an active role or were the victim of circumstances beyond your control. Even major successes that fell short of your expectations or that you felt were undeserved and were therefore disappointments should be included. Failures and disappointments in any aspect of your life will reveal the habits that didn't work for you in those situations.

If you can't list at least a dozen or two disappointing situations from your past, you're either not trying, your me-bias is working overtime, or you're only two years old and don't *have* much of a past.

Okay, go make your list.

Step 2: Select an experience from your bad news list and mentally relive that experience using the eight-sense experience technique.

Recent experiences are usually the ones to pick first. They're fresher in your memory and more indicative of the way you behave at this stage of your life and therefore more likely to reveal your blockers in their current form.

If there's an experience that you find you really don't want to deal with or has some other strong negative energy or unpleasant emotion connected with it, that's the one you should pick first because it's sure to reveal more about your blockages than your less troubling experiences.

The idea is to remember the experience you selected in as much detail as possible, and in doing so stimulate the unconscious associations related to the experience. The more detail you recall, the more associations you'll stimulate, and you need to do that in order to fully tap into your unconscious thinking and to bring as much of it as possible into your conscious awareness.

The best way to get maximum access to your unconscious mind is to have what I call an eight-sense reexperience. It's more than merely a memory. It's a mental recreation of the entire episode, one that reanimates all the sensory information and thinking that occurred in the actual experience. An eight-sense reexperience enables you to understand more clearly what was actually going on inside you at the time. It'll never be as intense as the actual experience was, but it'll be as close as you can get, and it'll be enough to reveal your blockers if you fully engage in it.

The eight-sense experience is fully described in Attachment B at the end of this book, and you should study it carefully. In a nutshell, it's this: your mind takes in information by way of the five senses of sight, hearing, touch, taste, and smell. It further uses thoughts, emotions, and bodily sensations to interpret and make sense of the world. The five senses, plus the three mental ways we process what our senses tell us, add up to an eight-sense experience. You have an eight-sense *re*experience by visualizing a past event as vividly and in as much detail as you can, remembering all the sights, sounds, textures, smells, and tastes as well as the thoughts, emotions, and bodily sensations that are associated with the experience.

So study Attachment B, use the eight-sense reexperience to process your memory of the bad news event you selected, and take your time with it. Make it as vivid and detailed as possible in your mind.

Step 3: Create a diagnostic ladder showing the reasons the experience was not as successful as you intended or expected it to be.

While the reexperience is fresh and vivid in your mind, immediately complete a diagnostic ladder, which is another tool that will help you penetrate deeply into the layers of your unconscious mind, where your blockers reside. The diagnostic ladder is an adaptation of a similar tool presented in Michael Ray's insightful book *The Highest Goal.*

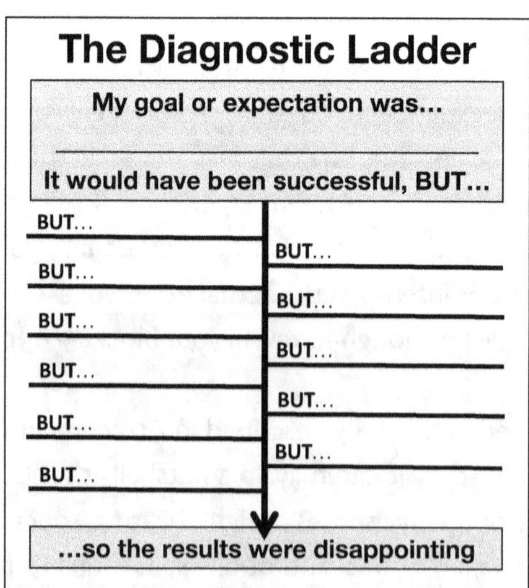

The diagnostic ladder asks you to identify the goal you were trying to achieve or the expectation that fell short and then, on the rungs of the ladder, fill in the reasons that you failed or fell short of your expectations. You'll probably find it easy to fill in three or four reasons that explain the disappointment, and you'll want to stop there, but don't stop. Push on and force yourself to fill in *all* of the blanks, even if you have to invent reasons you might not feel are quite right.

The reason you have to fill in all eleven blanks, even if you have to make up some answers and even if you are certain there were only one or two or three reasons, is that it pushes you past your conscious, top-of-mind thinking and past your rationalizations and more fully engages your unconscious mind.

Imagining answers or making up reasons for failure can seem silly or misleading, but it actually helps you penetrate your unconscious mind and lead to important (and true) discoveries. So fill in all eleven blanks.

Step 4: Probe the reasons in order to discover the habits of mind that blocked you, using the repeating question technique. Probe deeply in order to go beyond your cognitive biases and reveal the personality habits that contributed to your disappointment.

This step is the heart of the practice, but it can be tricky to get right. Take notes to keep track of your findings.

Pick one of the "but" reasons from the diagnostic ladder and explore it thoroughly, probing for the personality habits that got in your way. You have to ignore superficial excuses and dig deep into your conscious and unconscious thinking and behavior to get at the real blockers. This can be difficult because your mind may want to stop at the first thing you uncover (for instance, a cognitive bias) when in actuality, the underlying and real cause of the blockage may be some aspect of your personality.

Use the repeating question technique to probe each "but" reason. The repeating question technique is described in detail in Attachment C at the end of this book. Please study it carefully and pay close attention to the example.

In a nutshell, the repeating question technique is asking yourself, "What is it about this 'but' reason that blocked me?" Jot down your answer with key words or phrases that capture the essence of your answer. Then pick one of those key words or phrases (one that has some energy or importance to it or one that you'd rather avoid), and ask the same question about this idea: "What is it about [key word or phrase] that was blocking me?" Again, jot down the key words or phrases that come to you. Continue drilling down with the repeating question until you sense that you have reached the heart of the matter. You'll feel it as some kind of aha moment or a feeling of relief or satisfaction.

If you feel stumped or blocked at any level of repeating questions, it's a sign that you're unconsciously avoiding something. You'll need to break through that unconscious resistance. Push through it by repeatedly asking the question and, if necessary, speculating about answers that might be true of other people, even if you don't think they're true for you. Imagining what might be true for other people may seem wrong because you're tempted to think, "I'm not like other people." But the thought process, despite being imaginary, gains you access to your unconscious thinking and can lead you in the right direction. Again, jot down the key words/phrases. At some point, you'll have that aha moment, and you'll intuitively know that you've discovered what you were looking for.

Occasionally, you may still find yourself blocked and unable to break through. That's okay because you're going to be probing other "but" reasons from the diagnostic ladder, and even though you didn't get all the way to the bottom of this one, it's good preparation for your unconscious mind for the next ones you probe. Be patient with yourself.

Sometimes, you'll have a sense of completion without having discovered a personality trait responsible for the disappointment. That's because, in that instance, your personality may not have been the problem. It may have been one or more cognitive biases that blocked your success. Sense of completion is the key here. Sense of completion means an aha feeling, a sense of satisfaction, or some other positive response. If you feel blocked, resistant, are anxious about going further and are experiencing negative thoughts, intuitions, emotions, or bodily sensations that make you want to avoid further probing, it's a sign that you haven't gotten to the bottom of your probing, and you need to persist with the repeating questions. The signs can be subtle, so pay attention to your state of mind as you do this probing, and stick with it when your mind wants to resist going further.

I realize that this is all vague and touchy-feely. It has to be because this practice works differently in different people, and it relies on intuition and the unique associations that live in your mind and your mind only. You have to get in touch with your own inner workings and tune yourself in to the subtle ones, the ones you usually ignore or don't notice. The unconscious mind wants to stay unconscious, so you have to pay close attention to yourself and learn the ways that yours communicates with you. The language of the unconscious mind consists of emotions, bodily sensations, impressions, and intuitions. You'll have your own patterns to pay attention to. I can give you some hints, but because I don't know you, I can't tell you what your patterns might be. Fortunately, the more you engage in this practice, the better you'll become at doing it and the better you'll understand yourself, which is no small thing.

When you've probed each "but" reason and have a solid sense of completion about it, go on to the next one that draws your attention, especially one you would rather avoid.

Although you had to list at least eleven "but" reasons, you probably don't have to probe all of them. When do you know you're done? When the results of your probing become repetitious. You'll need to probe at least five "but" reasons to be sure you're not missing any important blockers, so five is the minimum. When you've probed five or more "but" reasons and the same habits of mind crop up again and again, you'll know you've mined this bad news experience for all of its secrets. So keep at it until either repetition sets in or you've probed all eleven reasons, but don't let yourself probe less than five.

At the end of this step, you should have five or more sheets of paper with key words and phrases scribbled on them, one sheet for each "but" reason you probed.

Step 5: Look for your patterns and priorities, and write the answer to this question: "What habits blocked me, and how did they interfere with my success?"

Review each of your key words and phrases sheets, looking for personality habits and cognitive biases that show up frequently or, if they only show up rarely, have major negative effects or feel important. I wish I had a formula for this process, but the only thing that seems to work is your own powers of observation and your intuition.

One warning: when you're looking for your patterns, don't merely count words. Yes, pay attention to the numbers; if a key word or phrase crops up many times, that means something, but so does your internal sense of importance, your intuition about yourself.

It's interesting, isn't it, that even when you're exploring your unconscious mind, the unconscious mind itself turns out to be your best tool?

Take another blank sheet of paper and write a quick note about what you've discovered about yourself and the habits of mind that blocked you when you had this bad news experience. Be specific, and be especially sure to write about the blockers that seemed to have created the strongest distortions of reality and contributed most strongly to the disappointing results of this experience. Attach this sheet to the front of your key words and phrases sheets.

Step 6: Go on to another experience on your bad news list, and do steps 2–5 again. Continue to do this until the results become repetitious and you have revealed all the personality habits that habitually block you.

At this point, you've thoroughly explored one experience from your life that didn't work out the way you wanted it to, and you've gotten a lot of valuable insights about the way your mind works and how your personality can get in your way. But you can't rely on one experience or even several experiences out of a lifetime of experiences to reveal the patterns that block you. You have to explore many experiences. How many? I don't know, but you will. When the exploration of your bad news experiences gets repetitious, when you see the same blocker habits of mind cropping up across many experiences, then you'll know how you block yourself.

In general, for most people, exploring five or ten experiences from relatively recent years will reveal their consistent patterns and allow them to identify the main ways they're blocking themselves. So think in terms of reviewing a half dozen to a dozen bad news experiences.

The last discovery step is to put it all together and begin a plan for unblocking yourself.

Step 7: Create your prioritized blocker list containing the personality habits that distort your thinking and behavior.

When you've completed exploring the necessary number of bad news experiences, you'll have many sheets of paper for each experience. That's your raw material. Let it sit for a day or so to allow your unconscious mind to integrate it all and then go back to your note sheets and put it all together in the form of a prioritized list of habits of mind, each of which has played a role in blocking you. That's your blocker list.

What do I mean by prioritized? The first item on your list should be the habit that had the greatest negative impact on your thoughts and actions across the greatest number of bad news life experiences. I define negative impact as distorted perceptions of reality. Be alert for: Beliefs that were wrong or at least uncertain. Emotional reactions that overwhelmed your perceptions and shaped ineffective or erroneous thoughts and actions on your part. Personality characteristics that weren't appropriate, meaning that they clouded your perceptions, limited your willingness to take the appropriate actions or motivated you to take inappropriate actions. All the stuff we talked about in the previous chapters.

If you're like most of us, your blocker list will be a mix of habits of thinking and habits of being. They might even be habits that are normally useful but which, in your bad news experiences, blocked you and produced disappointing results. The top item on the list will be the habit of thinking or personality trait that, across many bad news experiences, was the most significant contributor to the disappointing results or, said another way, blocked you more than any other habit on the list. Again, I can't give you objective criteria for choosing your most significant blockers because everyone's mind works in its own patterns; no formula works for everyone. I can assure you, however, that'll you know them when you see them.

Last, but not least, go back over your blocker list and identify each habit on the list as either a habit of thinking or personality habit. That's important because the process for converting cognitive biases into supporting habits is the two-question habit, which I covered in earlier chapters. It differs from and is simpler than the process for shifting your more deeply anchored personality habits, which I'll tell you about next.

Your blocker list is the end of your discovery process and the beginning of the what-are-you-going-to-do-about-it part of this book. The great thing about this discovery practice is that merely by getting deeply engaged in it (not simply going through the motions but really getting into it), the practice will change you for the better. Your unconscious mind pays attention to what you're doing even when what you're doing focuses on the unconscious mind itself, and it'll begin to think differently and better simply as a result of doing all this work. So you're already taking big steps toward breaking out of your goldfish bowl.

CHAPTER SEVENTEEN

What Can You Do About Dysfunctional Personality Habits?

Some Things to Think about Before You Convert Your Blocking Habits

Fortunately, it's possible to change personality habits, even the deep-seated ones that seem inborn, the ones that seem so *you*. Obstructive personality habits can be converted into productive ones, and the new habits that you need for success can be learned.

But you can't simply act differently. You have to change at the deep, unconscious, *real you* level. Some say "fake until you make it," but that simply disguises your underlying habits with artificial behavior in the hope that the artificiality will wear off and the behavior will eventually become genuine. It doesn't work. All you're doing is adding a new habit—the habit of acting. The underlying habits that the acting is attempting to camouflage still remain in place, and they'll reassert themselves, often at the worst possible time, when the stakes are important and stress is high.

For instance, don't you know people who are amazingly positive whatever the situation? And can't you immediately see which of them are genuinely positive and which ones have learned positivity techniques and think that makes them positive? The genuinely positive ones take on the world with an innate zest and genuine confidence while the others seem strained, unreal, and stressed, all the while smiling a dazzling smile and congratulating themselves on how very positive they are. You don't really trust them, do you? And unconsciously, they don't trust themselves. Their unconscious minds know the truth, and it shows; they can't hide it.

So instead of *acting* positive, confident, assertive, innovative, or any other desirable habit of mind, you need to learn how to build a foundation of supportive unconscious habits so that a productive attitude naturally emerges. That way you don't have to *act* positive, confident, assertive, or innovative because you *become truly* positive. You never have to act again. And that's where you're headed in this chapter, but before you get into the process by which you convert your blocking habits into supportive habits, let me say more about blocking habits.

Firstly, while you have many personality habits that collectively form your personality and shape your character, most people find that only a very few of them are important barriers to their success and only in certain situations. Two, three, or four of your personality habits will be blockers, rarely more. The point here is that even though you may have hundreds of personality habits, you'll only have to work on a small number of them. So it's not an insurmountable task.

Secondly, this whole process for converting blockers into productive personality habits is focused on you. If everyone were the same, I'd have offered a simple formula (like I did for cognitive biases) and advised you to follow that formula. But you are you, and your personality isn't like any other—not exactly. So your solutions have to be you-focused because anything else won't work. That means you'll have to explore your own inner landscape, and if you've ever done anything like this before or been close to others who have, you know it can be tricky and sometimes challenging, mainly because our minds are structured so that we see ourselves in an artificially favorable light—the me-bias—that so often blinds us to our own shortcomings.

So you not only have to discover what's true for you, but you also have to be open to a lot of surprising news about yourself, and it's sometimes stuff you don't want to know. The me-bias works the other way too. Some of you will have some falsely negative views of yourselves, such as "I'm not very creative," or "I'm a lousy sales-man," or "I'm not a detail person." Positive or negative, false beliefs about ourselves, and the habits of being they support, can be barriers against a lot of life's good stuff.

Before you embark on this journey, keep this in mind: don't expect it to be difficult. But don't expect it not to be. It will be what it is for you. Some people breeze through the process easily and quickly. Some work through it laboriously, stressed out and frustrated every step of the way. And some just don't get it and give up. The vast majority of normal, healthy people get a lot of aha moments about themselves, find some parts of the process difficult, and some parts easy, and look back on the journey as worthwhile and successful.

You're in control. You don't have to do any of this if you don't want to. And you can shift it around to work better if some part of the process isn't working for you. This whole book is simply a guideline built on mind/brain science and practices that have worked for others. But you're not others, and some parts of it may not work exactly right for you. So change it. When something doesn't work, you can and should do something else. So be open to other possibilities as you work through the process. As long as you follow the basic principles we've discovered and described in this book, you'll be okay.

And finally, don't expect a transformation. I don't believe in transformations. Transformation works for caterpillars and tadpoles, but not for people. Because the process is you-focused and because *you* are driving it, the results will be consistent with who you are and will reflect your own kind of person. I find that people who successfully come out the other side of the process don't say, "I'm a whole new person," but rather say something like, "I'm the same person I've always been, but things (my life, my relationships, my career) are working better for me."

Habit Conversion

The essence of habit conversion is to take advantage of the mind's natural habit formation process but to do it consciously, with the intention of replacing habits that aren't working for you. The essential elements of consciously forming a new habit are attention and repetition. You put your attention on the new habit you want to develop, and you practice it diligently until it becomes part of you. You saw a simple version of it with the 2Q habit introduced in an earlier chapter to deal with cognitive biases, but it's a bit more challenging for personality habits.

You can't simply identify a bad personality habit and decide not to do it any more. You have to replace it with a new habit, one that's compatible with your other habits of mind.

There's a saying that goes, "What you resist persists." It's true. Resisting a bad habit keeps that habit in your conscious and unconscious mind. It actually reinforces the undesirable habit. For example, if I tell you, "Don't think of a pink elephant," what happens? You think of a pink elephant; you can't help it. The harder you try not to think of a pink elephant, the longer the pink elephant stays in your mind. If you want to eliminate the image of the pink elephant, you have to think of something else. Instead of resisting the pink elephant, you replace it with, say, the image of a unicorn. Look at what just this moment happened in your own mind. Didn't the image of a unicorn flash into your mind, and for that moment, didn't the pink elephant disappear? So the basic principle of habit conversion is this: don't try to resist or eliminate the old habit; *replace* it with something better.

Part of the problem of persistent bad habits is that they're always stimulated (triggered) by something, and that something is almost always either unconscious or unnoticed. The way to convert a blocking habit into an effective habit is to identify the trigger and make yourself conscious of it so you can use it as an alert to tell you when to engage in new behavior to replace the old habit. After you do it enough times, the trigger will automatically and unconsciously stimulate the new habit instead of the old, and you'll have successfully converted the old habit, not by rejecting it, but by replacing it.

Let me illustrate by continuing the example of Jerry, whom you met earlier. Recall that Jerry had developed the lifelong personality habit of conflict avoidance based on the way he learned to cope with his father's anger as a child. As you may remember, over time as Jerry grew into manhood, avoidance became the unconscious pattern—a personality habit—for the way he dealt with all real and imagined conflicts.

> *Every time Jerry got into a confrontation with someone or imagined that a confrontation might develop, he became tense and got a tight feeling in his gut. Whenever the tight feeling happened, Jerry would relieve the tension by moving away from the situation, or if he couldn't physically move away, he would withdraw mentally by numbing out, becoming confused, or simply going blank. Others saw it as changing the subject, going along to get along, or disengaging from the discussion by going silent, none of which helped move the situation forward to a useful solution or decision.*

> *His behavior was so habitual that he no longer noticed the tightness in his gut and didn't even realize that he was avoiding real or imagined conflict. If you pointed it out to him, he simply rationalized his behavior by saying, "Well, I just didn't have anything to contribute to the discussion," or "I was very interested in the discussion, and I could see merit in both sides of the argument, but I had no position on it, so I just listened."*

> *When Jerry used the discovery process and found that conflict avoidance was at the top of his blocker list, his first reaction was shock and embarrassment. His second reaction was "I've got to do something about that."*

> *When I helped him mentally recall and relive several situations in which his conflict avoidance was an important contributor to his failure or disappointment, he became aware that, in every instance, he always felt a tension in his gut just before his conflict avoidance habit took charge of him. That gave us a way to change this long-standing and unproductive habit of mind.*

He devised a way to avoid his avoidance. Rather than disengaging and withdrawing, he would simply ask questions. He'd use curiosity and questioning to stay engaged and contribute to a positive result rather than merely escaping from the situation. He had a natural curiosity, so asking questions gave him a nonconflictual way to interrupt the old habit and stay engaged. And in those few instances when conflict actually did result, his conscious awareness and intention to stay engaged, combined with the questioning approach, gave him a useful and productive way to work his way through the conflict.

In short, he primed himself to notice his gut tension so he could use it as an alert to short-circuit his disengagement and to trigger a better way of behaving in a potentially conflictual situation. When real-time situations happened, he was able to notice the gut alert and consciously shift his old habit into the new questioning behavior.

Eventually, with both real-life and mental practice, the gut tension became an unconscious trigger to the questioning habit instead of the withdrawing one. In just a few weeks, the old habit disappeared because his new habit eliminated the sense of threat in these situations, which eliminated the tension. It became natural for him to become productively involved in finding solutions and helping to eliminate the potential for conflict. His withdrawal and avoidance shifted into engagement and problem solving—a whole new habit of being for him. Is it any wonder that his life improved from that point onward?

I hope you find it reassuring that this process depends on the natural ways your mind functions. You don't have to learn anything new; you just have to take advantage of what your mind already does by nature and do it consciously rather than unconsciously. All you do is consciously notice your triggers and intentionally move into a new behavior of your own creation, one that's in tune with who you are and that will be more productive than the old habit. Your mind is already equipped to form and reform habits. All I'm doing is helping you learn how to do it consciously, deliberately, and in service of your own success rather than as an unconscious response to your lifelong conditioning.

CHAPTER EIGHTEEN

The Personality Habit Conversion Process

For many people, the process of converting personality habits can be a bit tricky, so I'm going to ask you to ease into it. The first thing I'd like you to do is look at the overview below, which summarizes the process. It'll give you the lay of the land for what we'll be doing next. After that, I'll walk you through each step of the process, and after that, if you're willing, you'll begin to reconstruct your own blocker habits so they'll serve you better.

Overview

The Personality Habit Conversion Process

1. Select a blocker habit from the list of personality habits that block you.

2. Select a bad news experience in which that blocker habit was a problem for you. Mentally relive it through the eight-sense reexperience so that you fully engage your unconscious thinking about the experience. Make sure you identify the trigger that stimulates the blocker habit.

3. Choose/design a new supportive habit.

    •   For habits of thinking (cognitive biases), use the 2Q technique.

- For personality habits, create a new, supportive way of being. This is the way you believe you should have behaved at that time and should behave in the future in order to be more effective and appropriate. It should be consistent with your personality, and, if possible, it should take advantage of your other habits of mind. In other words, it should be authentic.

4. Mentally practice the new, improved habit the eight-sense *preexperi*ence way, and engage the new habit in real-time situations whenever they occur in the ordinary course of your life.

5. Practice to completion.

That's the overview. Now let's get you engaged with the real thing. Keep in mind that you'll be clumsy with the process at first. It will feel weird and unnatural, but with practice, it'll all become comfortable and you'll get good at it. Here's the detailed process.

Step 1: Select a blocker habit from your blocker list.

The first time you use this conversion process, select secondary blocker habits to work on. By secondary, I mean habits that contributed to your disappointments and failures but weren't the most important habits, the ones that drove the experience. These would be habits that you didn't prioritize as first, second, or third on your blocker list. The reason should be obvious; you'll get the best results from the conversion process after you've had some practice with it. The highest priority blockers are the ones that will be most important to convert, so practice on a secondary habit before taking on the ones that drive your unsuccessful experiences. If you only discovered one blocker habit, then, of course, work on that one.

Step 2: Select a bad news experience in which that blocker habit was active. Mentally relive it the eight-sense reexperience way.

When you did your discovery work, you explored a number of bad news experiences from your life, experiences in which things didn't turn out as you wanted or expected. Go back to your bad news experiences and pick one in which the blocker you selected played a role in blocking your success.

You'll need to relive that experience as vividly as you can. As you learned in the discovery process, the eight-sense *re*experience is the best way to do that. As you did before, close your eyes, relax, and mentally relive the experience, regenerating as much as you can in your mind of the sights, sounds, smells, tastes, textures, thoughts, emotions, and bodily sensations that you experienced at the time of the actual experience. You've already done this at least once, so it should be easy.

Step 3: Identify the trigger point and establish your alert.

While your reexperience is still vivid in your mind, look for the point at which your blocker habit was triggered. It'll be the point in time just before the habit took hold and locked you into your automatic way of thinking or being.

This can be tricky because these triggers often go unnoticed in real time, and they can be subtle. Also, you never know if it's a thought, emotion, or bodily sensation that's associated with the point at which the habit takes hold, so as you're reliving the experience, you have to pay close attention to what's going on within you and around you during the moment the habit is triggered. A trigger could be a momentary hesitancy, an instant of anxiety that you normally wouldn't notice, a spark of annoyance or irritation, a little tingle of apprehension, a flash of impatience, a hint of fear, or a thought such as "Oh no, not again"—anything you notice about yourself, your thoughts and emotions, or even the situation around you that occurs just before you go into the habitual behavior.

This is another of those things that's unique to you. Again, I can't give you a formula, just some hints about what to look for. The rule is that it must be something that you can prime yourself to notice so that it will alert you to stay conscious and aware and to intentionally interrupt the blocker habit and divert yourself into a different thinking pattern or a better way of being.

In the example of Jerry dealing with his conflict aversion, his trigger was that he always either had a strong desire to withdraw or go silent or a need to be elsewhere, and it was always accompanied by tension in his gut. He primed himself by deciding that when he noticed the gut tension, it would remind him to engage in the new replacement habit. In the early days of habit reformation, he had to consciously think about this, but the more he did it, the more the old gut tension lost its power to trigger the old behavior and became the trigger for the new habit. Instead of triggering his old blocker, the gut tension became the signal (his alert) to stay engaged and attempt to improve the situation rather than merely avoid it.

Having identified your alert, what do you do about it? How do you devise an improved habit of mind to take the place of the ineffective one?

Step 4: Choose/design a new supportive habit.

Recall that on your blocker list, you identified each blocker habit as either a cognitive bias or a personality habit. I asked you to do that because the two kinds of habits require different conversions. As you saw in the previous chapter, cognitive biases are all fixed by the 2Q habit: What's Reality A? What are the possibilities?

You have to be more clever about habits of being. For them, you need to create a new supportive personality habit to replace or modify the blocker.

There's a secret to successfully converting blockers, and it's this: the new habit must be compatible with the way your mind works, not simply some artificial and uncomfortable way of thinking or being that you have to force upon yourself.

For instance, if you were to think, "I'll be just like the Dalai Lama, peaceful and positive," but your normal habits of mind are more action-based and passionate, then the replacement habit won't take hold and won't replace the old habit. It'll be like acting positive when you aren't truly positive.

Think again about Jerry and his conflict aversion. The new habit for him was based on the fact that he was a genuinely curious person with a sincere desire to help make a situation better, and his constellation of normal habits tended to support that state of mind. Real or imagined conflict threw him into withdrawal/avoidance, and because that was not his usual state of mind, it made his discomfort with conflict even greater.

When Jerry primed himself to notice his gut tension and use it as an alert to interrupt his blocker behavior, he used that awareness to trigger the conscious intention to hang in there and to do so by asking questions and working toward solutions. In other words, he took advantage of his normal productive state of mind—curiosity and helpfulness—and used that as the foundation of his new effective habit. Whenever he felt the gut tension and the desire to withdraw, he consciously and intentionally stuck with it and substituted questioning and curiosity as the preferred behavior. At first, it was awkward and uncomfortable, but because it fit with the other aspects of his personality, it quickly became a new habit even though it was stimulated by the same old trigger. Eventually, the gut tension disappeared because conflictual situations lost their threat and became events that stimulated his curiosity, which came natural to him.

Here's a thought experiment for you that might help you understand how you might go about creating a new, more effective habit of being for yourself.

> *Imagine that the habit you need to change is that you're overly impulsive. Most of your bad news experiences were driven by impulsiveness, which causes you to jump to conclusions and act immediately rather than being more thoughtful and seeking the best course of action.*

Imagine also that you've discovered that the trigger for your impulsivity is the urge to get results quickly, and the urge has a physical component, which is a bodily sensation of a pleasant sort of tingling in your solar plexus—an urge to swing into action—which you've noticed takes place immediately before you make significant decisions and act on them.

Like most impulsive people, you probably trust your intuition more than your analytical thinking. You're probably not aware that the best decisions are the result of a combination of intuitive and analytical thinking working in tandem. You're also an action-oriented person, and that's a good thing that you wouldn't want to suppress.

You can use your natural bias for action as the foundation for a new, more effective habit of being than your impulsiveness. You might do that by redirecting your action bias toward finding the best possible alternative rather than acting on the first thing that occurs to you. In other words, you redefine "action" to mean the search for the best solution, and you redefine "impulsivity" as the intuitive need to get the best result rather than the need to swing into action as quickly as possible.

If you try to establish the habit of "slow down and think," that'll run counter to the constellation of habits that you've built over your lifetime that compels you into (usually premature) action. You won't be able to do it. It'll feel awful to slow down, and you'll feel like you're wasting precious time dithering about the situation; it'll feel like paralysis by analysis. But if you redirect your energy and action bias into finding the right solution rather than the immediate solution, and if you trust your whole mind—both your intuition and your analytical thinking—you'll be able to create a whole new way of making decisions, and it'll be strengthened by your action bias and your trust in your intuition.

Your thought process might go something like this:

I learned in my discovery process that most of the poor decisions I've made in my life happened when I was too impulsive, too action biased. I used to think that my intuition was reliable and that I was a quick decision-maker for that reason. But when I reviewed the poor decisions I've made in my life, it became clear that I was merely jumping to conclusions, believing them to be right. And at the time, they felt right, although in most cases, they later proved to have been wrong and ultimately led to disappointments.

But I can't simply become a deliberate, slow, overly cautious decision-maker. That would drive me crazy, and I'm not sure I could even do it. However, I can see the possibility of redirecting my action bias into an aggressive search for the best course of action and verify my intuition with some analytical thinking. I could look at it like this: my first and immediate decision would be to search for the best course of action, and my second decision would be to aggressively put that course of action into effect.

As I think about it, I can see that I'd be converting impulsiveness into assertiveness or even aggressiveness, but thoughtful rather than careless aggressiveness. Instead of wasting time, I'd be making the best possible use of my time, and emotionally it would still feel action-based, not inert or lazy. The best part of this approach is that it feels like me, and it takes advantage of what has always felt like one of my greatest strengths.

It's all simply a shift of perspective, isn't it? But it's a genuine shift, not an act, and emotionally it feels right because it's true to what feels like my basic nature. That's because it meshes rather than conflicts with some of my other important habits of mind. It's not transformation. It's realignment of an ineffective habit of mind so that it meshes with the effective parts of my personality and my effective habits of thinking.

Designing the best replacement habit requires a lot of willingness to be honest, open, and objective about yourself and to allow for a lot of new possibilities that you may not have considered. It's all part of becoming more conscious, more aware, and more intentional about your life. It's ultimately about overcoming the normal supremacy of unconscious thinking and being.

To summarize, you'll need to devise a replacement habit that taps into your authentic personality and takes advantage of other existing but productive habits, and you'll need to prime yourself so that when you experience the trigger, it'll alert you to consciously initiate the new, more effective way of being.

Step 5: Preexperience the new, improved habit using the eight-sense preexperience technique.

If you're like me, you're probably thinking, "How the heck can I do that? Yes, I can imagine a replacement habit, but how can I get it into my unconscious mind and make it work?"

Once again, you'll need to use the eight-sense experience, in fact two of them: an eight-sense *re*experience, followed by an eight-sense *pre*experience. I'll walk you through it. First, you have an eight-sense reexperience of a time when your existing habit didn't work well for you. You should pick one of the same past experiences you used when you were discovering your blockers list because it'll be familiar to you, fresh in your mind, and you'll know what the trigger/alert was. As you're reexperiencing the event, you'll come to the point at which it was triggered. This is where the reexperience stops and the preexperience begins, the point at which you switch from memory to imagination. Visualize a way you could have and should have handled the event to produce a better result, and visualize yourself as if you had behaved this new way instead of what you actually did.

In other words, visualize success instead of disappointment, and try to live it in your imagination as if you had done it in real time, as if it had actually occurred in your past. You may have to try out a few different scenarios in your mind to find one that your intuition and logic tell you will work and will also feel like you. Remember, you need to find a new habit that will mesh with your personality, one that you believe will work, but also one that is compatible with who you are. It might take a few different preexperiences to find one that will be authentic, and I can't tell you what that authentic one might be. I can tell you that it'll be the one that feels less awkward than the others.

Anything you imagine yourself doing that's different from your old habit (the one you need to replace) will feel different and probably somewhat strange, but the one that resonates with the authentic you will give you a sense of rightness, a sense of "this is it." Go with that. If it turns out not to be right or if you later discover a better way of being, you can always shift to the better way as soon as you discover it. In fact, as you mentally practice the new habit, you should continually be alert for better possibilities and adopt them as they occur to you. As you practice, you'll settle in to the way that works best for you.

Let me say a bit more about visualization and mental rehearsal to reassure you that this technique of preexperiencing is much more than wishful thinking and playing pretend. A preexperience or visualization is trying something new on for size without actually risking failure or embarrassment. You'll never create a mental experience that's as intense as one you actually live, of course, but visualization using the eight-sense reexperience or preexperience is the next best thing. The reason for using visualization at all is that you can make great progress yet do it all in your mind where it's safe, where you can't make mistakes, and where there are no risks, no embarrassment, and no failures or negative consequences.

Let me give you an example. In college, I was a diver on the varsity swimming team. The first thing my coach taught me was visualization. For every dive, without exception, I was to imagine myself performing the dive perfectly. Only after that mental rehearsal was I allowed to mount the diving board and do the dive. When learning a new dive, I mentally practiced dozens if not hundreds of times in my mind before attempting the dive for the first time. The scarier and more difficult the dive, the more I practiced it mentally before diving.

Diving is a physical habit, but any habit can be imagined and practiced by visualization with no risk of failure, no embarrassment, and the more you visualize it, the more you become accustomed to it. When you finally do it for real, it feels familiar and flows much more easily than if you tried it without mental rehearsal.

What my diving coach didn't know and what I've learned over the years is that the eight-sense approach works best because it engages all the senses and all of the conscious and unconscious mental associations (head, heart, and gut) that make the internal experience as real as possible. Nothing is happening in the real, external world yet, but in your mind, you're establishing new neural pathways that will have real-world consequences. Just as I once did when learning a new dive, you're mentally rehearsing something you've never done, so that when you actually do it, it will work for you.

Step 6: Practice to completion.

When you've identified your new replacement habit of being, then visualize (preexperience) the new behavior several times daily; rehearse it in your mind. Adjust and revise it mentally whenever you feel that you need to in order to get it right. And be on the alert for real-world situations to put the new habit into actual practice.

Mental practice is all well and good, but what you're after is results in the real world, when real-life situations occur. And that's what you'll do. Rehearse the new behavior mentally several times daily in the safety of your mind so that when situations occur in real life, you'll do what you've mentally rehearsed.

Real life is the acid test. If in real life the new habit needs adjusting, then adjust it. Find the behavior that works best for you, and then diligently and consciously do it at all opportunities. And continue your visualization.

How long do you do this? Do it until you do it automatically, without consciously thinking about it. At that point in time, and no sooner, it'll have become a new habit of mind and will need no further rehearsal because it'll have become part of who you are.

If you find yourself thinking, "Now I've got it. I know how to consciously trigger the new habit," it's proof that you haven't yet fully eliminated the blocker. You've just superseded the old habit from time to time with conscious intention. The very fact that you've consciously thought about the old habit—even to avoid it—means that it's still alive in you and not fully replaced by the new habit. What needs to happen is that you *consciously* engage the new habit every time you're triggered and be diligent about doing it every time. Eventually, you'll forget to put your conscious intention on it, and the new habit, with no further conscious intention, becomes unconscious and asserts itself whenever the trigger occurs. It won't occur to you to think about it; you'll automatically do it.

I can't tell you how many times people have told me, "I get it," believing that they need only decide on a new habit and be aware of the trigger, and that's all that's necessary. Just because you know the trigger and the new habit in your conscious mind doesn't mean that it's anchored in your unconscious mind. In fact, it's not. Until the new habit itself becomes unconscious and your conscious mind is no longer even aware that that trigger is sliding you into the new habit, the new habit is not yet established. You're still at the point at which you can snap back into your old habit.

When the new habit is familiar and easy to engage, I guarantee that you'll be tempted to let it go at that and stop practicing. Don't stop. Continue practicing until you forget about it and it becomes automatic. It's the way you were conditioned into your existing habits of mind, and it's the *only* way you'll successfully convert blocker habits into new ones that work better for you.

I have to repeat something one more time: initially, you can expect discomfort, forgetfulness, and, in some cases, fear of failure or embarrassment. That's why mental practice—visualization through the eight-sense preexperience—is so important. You get to practice in the privacy of your own mind, where there are no witnesses, no risks, and where you can experiment with no consequences while still getting the benefits of practice and self-conditioning.

Do not shortcut this process.

Final Thoughts About Habit Conversion

So far in this book, all we've been doing is clearing away the barriers to success by helping you to identify your cognitive biases and blocker habits so that you can learn how to think and act more realistically, more consciously, and more intentionally.

Your thinking should improve dramatically and quickly as you discover your blocker habits and convert them to more productive ways of thinking and being. As you already know, it's an awkward process in the beginning, but you get better at it over time. As you use the discovery and conversion processes, they too will become automatic and unconscious habits of mind. Stick with it, and you'll become a clear thinker with a productive personality, and it'll become your innate, basic nature, not some skill that you've adopted. It'll be a permanent upgrade of who you are—not a transformation but a better you.

You may have noticed something important about this whole process. The 2Q technique for converting cognitive biases plus the blocker conversion process are actually creating a whole new personality habit—three of them, really: the habits of openness, objectivity, and creativity. You're opening up to a broader range of possibilities and other points of view. You're becoming more objective. And you're engaging your curiosity, imagination, and creativity. You're genuinely becoming a more open, objective, curious, and creative person.

Does that sound familiar? It should. Openness, objectivity, and creativity are the traits of Original Mind. In addition to installing new, productive, success-based habits of mind, what you're really doing with all of this work is reengaging your

Original Mind—not the Original Mind of an infant, but that of a mature, clear-thinking adult.

I realize all of this is a lot of work. And it's challenging because you're reengaging some of the more painful or sensitive experiences in your life, digging into some deeply buried parts of your mind, and confronting a lot of things about yourself that might be uncomfortable. The problem is that this is one of those things that's inherently awkward, at least in the beginning. Your mind is enormously complex, and it's taken you all of your lifetime to build the habits of mind that inhabit your head, including the ones that are blocking you.

It won't take you a lifetime to release your blockages and establish better habits, but it may take weeks, possibly longer for some of you, and you have to *engage* in the process or it won't work.

It's not positive thinking, it's not fake it until you make it, it's not slogans or formulas, and it's not opening yourself up to the universe to make things right. It's you reshaping your mind.

It all comes back to "be all you can be," doesn't it?

META HABITS

CHAPTER NINETEEN

Core Purpose: The Source of Deep Motivation

Purpose and Motivation

All the gurus of leadership and personal development recognize that every person has a powerful inner drive that's usually unnoticed and unconscious yet still influential to everything we do in life. Renowned author and lecturer Tony Robbins calls it one's sense of "ultimate destiny." Michael Gerber, pioneering business coach and author of the best-selling E-Myth books, calls it "Primary Aim." Steven Covey, best-selling author of *The 7 Habits of Highly Effective People,* identifies it as a spiritual drive for meaning and contribution. Michael Ray, author of *Creativity in Business* and creator of the Stanford University course in business creativity, calls it the "Greatest Goal." Others have different names for it, but they all recognize that it exists and that it's an important source of motivation and power. I call it "Core Purpose."

We all have a lot of things in life that motivate us, but Core Purpose is the deepest and most meaningful. It's the source of our most enduring motivation. If you can see how your decisions and actions contribute to accomplishing your Core Purpose, then you've made a connection that will sustain you when the going gets tough and you're tempted to quit or take the easy way out.

Everyone has a Core Purpose, and it's different for everyone. Yet most people aren't aware that (a) they even have a Core Purpose, much less what it is, and (b) how important it is to live their lives in ways that are in harmony with their Core Purposes.

A Deep Sense of Purpose, Not a Reaction to Needs

I'm going to show you a process for discovering your Core Purpose in a moment, but first you need to know a bit about human motivation and why Core Purpose stands apart from other kinds of motivation. Bear with me while I get a bit pedantic; it'll just take a moment.

In 1943, Abraham Maslow published a paper entitled "A Theory of Human Motivation" in which he observed that people are motivated to fulfill their needs, and those needs exist in a hierarchy in which the more basic needs must be satisfied before the higher needs can become motivators. In other words, if you're starving, you probably aren't motivated to join the country club, but if you're healthy and well-fed, and you feel safe and secure, then the need to be accepted and belong to a desirable group will emerge as strong motivators for you.

The needs Maslow identified (from the most basic to the more elevated) were physiological (survival, being the most basic), safety/security, love/belonging, esteem/accomplishment, self-actualization, and self-transcendence, which Maslow added in later years. The need for self-transcendence is the domain of Core Purpose, and you'll see in a moment how it differs from the other needs and why that's important to you.

Here's a summary of Maslow's hierarchy, with needs listed from the most basic at the bottom of the list to the highest at the top:

Maslow's Hierarchy of Needs	
SELF-TRANSCENDENCE	Higher goals, outside of the self. Service to the "greater self" or humanity. Not a need but a sense of purpose. (Outer-directed)
SELF-ACTUALIZATION	The urge to "be all you can be." (Self-referenced)
ESTEEM/ACHIEVEMENT	The need for status, recognition, accomplishment. (Self-referenced)
LOVE/BELONGING	The need for affiliation with others and groups; relationships. (Self-referenced)
SAFETY/SECURITY	The need to be safe and secure. (Self-referenced)
PHYSIOLOGICAL	The need for sustenance and comfort; physical needs, such as food, shelter, etc. The so-called "survival" needs. (Self-referenced)

Maslow identified self-transcendence as the highest need, but this is where I depart from his theory. My education, bolstered by my experience in business, in the military, and in family matters, has shown me that self-transcendence is a motivator whether or not lower-level needs have been satisfied. In other words, when the stakes are important, we humans are capable of putting others ahead of ourselves and making sacrifices for the greater good. We can be self-transcendent at any time and in any situation as long as our sense of purpose is triggered. We can also be self-indulgent, selfish, and self-referenced while ignoring our higher sense of purpose. When we're reacting to our needs, we're self-referenced; when we're acting in the interests of others, groups or individuals—that is, self-transcendent—then we're outer-directed. And it's all unconscious until we make ourselves aware and until we learn to balance needs satisfaction with self-transcendence.

So what exactly is self-transcendence, how does Core Purpose fit into this picture, and what does it mean for you?

Self-transcendence is not so much a need as it is a sense of purpose. The difference is important because you *react* to your needs by responding, usually unconsciously, to the urges they generate. Reacting to needs is self-referenced—selfish, if you like. There's nothing wrong with that; we all need to take care of ourselves and seek personal pleasures and satisfactions. But if that's all there is, then our lives are hollow indeed. It's self-transcendence, which is outer-directed, that brings greater meaning to us, and it improves not only our lives but also the lives of others within our circles of influence.

The trick is to find balance so that you're serving yourself while also serving a purpose greater than yourself.

We all have an innate, inborn self-transcendence (we can't *not* have it), but it takes different forms for each of us, and it plays out differently in each of our lives. That's what this chapter is all about: discovering *your* individual form of self-transcendence.

You can't become truly successful without bringing your self-transcendence into balance with your needs, and you can't do that unless you discover your particular form of self-transcendence, your Core Purpose. Having done that, you can consciously use that knowledge to guide your important decisions. It's important for your happiness and sense of achievement that what you do is somehow connected to your Core Purpose.

How to Discover Your Core Purpose

Your Core Purpose isn't always easy to identify. Mine wasn't. Some people discover theirs immediately; others struggle to find theirs.

It's often helpful to look at Core Purpose as the answer to three questions:

1. What impact do I want to have in the world?

2. What's right for me to do, and what's wrong?

3. What kind of person do I want to be?

Core Purpose is most easily discovered in cooperation with an experienced advisor or coach, but there is an abbreviated process you can use by yourself to get some understanding of your Core Purpose. Here are the steps of that process.

A Process for Identifying Your Core Purpose

1. Look to your own past and make a list of those experiences that were meaningful or important to you.

    Meaningful doesn't mean happiness, joy, pride, or admiration from others, although those might have been part of the experience. Meaningful means that you found the experience deeply satisfying and you derived a sense of accomplishment or contribution from it. The experience might be something you did, or it could be something that impressed you deeply from some other source, such as a book, movie, an event you witnessed, or the behavior of someone you respect or admire. The only rule is that it must have been deeply meaningful to you. Make a list of as many of those experiences as you can remember.

2. Choose one experience from your list that was especially meaningful to you.

3. Mentally relive that experience in as much detail as possible. Use the eight-sense reexperience technique to put you in touch with your unconscious mind.

4. Focus on what was meaningful about the experience.

    Emotions are an important guide. The stronger emotions associated with satisfaction and meaning are clues to Core Purpose. You have to dig deep within yourself, so don't be satisfied with your first impression of the experience. Identify as specifically as you can what was meaningful. The repeating question technique will help you drill down to what's true for you. Write down some key words to describe it.

5. Select another meaningful experience and repeat the process (steps 3 and 4).

    You should review at least five experiences. Ten would be better; more would be better yet. One or two experiences don't reveal a pattern, and it's the pattern that will lead you to your Core Purpose. Keep your notes on separate sheets for each experience.

6. Look for patterns.

    When you have relived your meaningful experiences, lay out all of your note sheets and look for the patterns. There's no formula for this. It's completely subjective, and you are the only person qualified to do it because you are the only one capable of knowing what's meaningful for you.

7. Write a short statement beginning with, "My Core Purpose is …"

    If you seem to have more than one possible Core Purpose, write statements for each, and then compare them, observing your inner reactions carefully. One statement will have more emotional weight than the other(s), and that statement will lead you to your Core Purpose. Or you might find an even deeper sense of meaning that underlies the multiple statements.

8. Condense the idea of your Core Purpose into a word or short phrase but no more than a short sentence.

    The phrase might be meaningless or silly to others, but it should trigger the full sense of Core Purpose in your own mind. I once had a great friend whose Core Purpose was contained in the statement, "Life is a chair of bowlies," which was a play on the old saying, "Life is a bowl of cherries."

Yes, it sounds frivolous to you and me, but it was exactly right and deeply meaningful to her. Remember, you don't have to share your Core Purpose with anyone else, but you absolutely *must* discover it for yourself. If your statement sounds silly, so what?

The central idea is to make your Core Purpose conscious so it can guide your decisions and actions in life and business. One practical way to do that is to use the three questions mentioned earlier and apply them to important decisions in your life while keeping your Core Purpose in your conscious awareness:

1. Will [the decision or action] result in the impact I want to have?

2. Is [the decision or action] the right thing to do?

3. Does the [decision or action] reflect the kind of person I want to be?

Don't be confused by money. Money can be central to all of the lower-level needs, and it can be a tool for serving your Core Purpose, but the accumulation of money is never your Core Purpose. Money buys you food, shelter, etc. and is key to satisfying survival needs. It also buys you protection and safety from threats, and the accumulation of wealth provides a great sense of security. Money also buys you access to and makes you more welcome in many social settings and groups. It is a scorecard with which you can measure esteem needs like competence, status, and achievement, and some of your self-actualization (be all you can be) needs. Money never satisfies the need, but it *is* a tool that can be useful at all levels of need.

There's a potential problem in this discovery process. Your self-referenced needs (survival, security, belonging, self-actualization, etc.) can overshadow your Core Purpose. Not only that, but some needs can masquerade as Core Purpose, especially the social and esteem needs.

So you must be sure that the Core Purpose you discover is true self-transcendence and not a lower-level need that you mistake for Core Purpose. How do you do that? You test your thinking by noticing if it is self-referenced (focused on you) or other-referenced (focused on others or on a cause bigger than yourself).

Here's an example from the world of business coaching:

> *Caroline, a business coach trainee, had identified her Core Purpose as the following: to become the preeminent business coach in the nation. It sounded grand. Certainly the nation's preeminent business coach would be in a position to bring greater meaning and make major contributions.*

> *Caroline's trainer, Fred (an experienced business coach who was mentoring new coaches), suspected that Caroline was on the right track but was being misled by her lower-level needs. The following (abbreviated) conversation got Caroline to her true Core Purpose.*

Fred: *Let's test your Core Purpose to be sure it's right. What is it about "becoming the nation's preeminent business coach" that's meaningful to you?*

Caroline: *Well, it would mean that I would be helping business people have better lives, and the better I did it, the better their lives would be and the more respect I'd get for making it happen.*

Fred: *So the respect part is what's most important?*

Caroline: *Well, sure, the respect part would be good, but the part that would be really meaningful would be knowing that I had improved so many lives. Having a great reputation would feel good, and status is very important to me, but more importantly, it would bring more people to me so I could help them.*

Fred: *So it's the "helping people have better lives" part that's the most important thing?*

Caroline: *Yes. I want the status, but it would be hollow if that's all there was.*

Fred: *What about the business people part? You only want to improve the lives of business people?*

Caroline: *Well, no, but my expertise is in business and coaching, so that's the most realistic path for me.*

Fred: *So "improving peoples' lives" is the core of it, isn't it? And you focus on business people because that's where you believe you can be most effective?*

Caroline: *Exactly.*

Fred: *It sounds to me like your Core Purpose is rich but simple: to improve people's lives. You may do it in the arena of business because that's where your skill set lies, but in your heart of hearts, you seem to want to help make peoples' lives better, and the more people you can impact, whether they're business people or not, the better.*

Caroline: *Yeah. Y'know, you're right!* [Caroline's eyes opened wide at this point, and she became more animated.]

Fred: *Now, don't let me put words in your mouth. Look inside yourself. Does it feel right for you to say, "My Core Purpose is to make peoples' lives better"?*

Caroline: *My Core Purpose is to make peoples' lives better. That's it! It makes sense, and I don't have any of those little intuitive signals that happen when something isn't right for me.*

What's the point? The point is that when you're identifying your Core Purpose, don't be mislead by the lower-level needs. Stay focused on your highest sense of purpose, and use the repeating question technique to dig deeply within yourself until you have the solid sense that you've found it.

A word of caution for you skeptics—and this was true of me before I got wise to my own Core Purpose—this is no airy-fairy New Age head-trip. It's a true source of motivation and commitment. It's what makes your work a joy rather than drudgery. When what you do serves your inner sense of purpose, you do it well with energy and commitment. So please don't look at Core Purpose as simply another power of positive thinking gimmick. It's a real source of strength and motivation. I hope you'll take full advantage of the power it can release in you.

CHAPTER TWENTY

Strategic Thinking

Seeing What's Possible and How to Get It Done

What Is Strategic Thinking?

Strategic thinking is the ability to understand the underlying principles and dynamics of a situation and to put that understanding to use managing, planning, and/or evaluating it. It further includes the ability to see the big picture simultaneously with the details as well as the ability to see beyond habitual rules and conventional wisdom and to discover new principles, rules, and ways of behaving.

Strategic thinking enables you to formulate a vision, a mental picture of what is to be achieved, and then to create a plan for achieving that vision. It enables you to understand complex phenomena and to articulate them clearly in words and images. It includes the ability to identify opportunities and possibilities as well as threats and constraints and to understand the need for change or the need not to change.

Strategic thinking comes with practice; we're probably all born with the aptitude, but if we don't put it to use, we never develop it. Strategic thinking requires fuel—it feeds on information. The best strategic thinkers are information junkies.

Strategic thinking is a meta habit comprised of five cognitive habits: holism, whole mind thinking, innovation, double vision, and curiosity.

Holism

Strategic thinkers see things holistically, as an organism and not a collection of parts. A business, for instance, is an integrated whole, not an assembly of marketing, finance, human resources, and other parts. Similarly, a human being is not merely an assembly of lungs, legs, teeth, and fingers. Yes, you can look at a business or a person as a collection of parts, but when you do, you cut yourself off from truly understanding what it is to be a business or what it is to be human.

Strategic thinkers see and understand the connectedness, the interdependence, the integrated nature of the world and the people in it. When they consider a problem in one area, they also consider the impact of that problem on everything connected with it. When they teach children, work on their jobs, develop relationships with others, make important decisions—when they do anything—they are aware of the broader implications of their actions.

The holistic view of life is something that most people never quite understand. They live their lives in a sea of disconnected, isolated parts and have little understanding of how people and things interconnect, interrelate, and are interdependent.

But modern life is inherently complex. It's not made up of unrelated things, people, and events. You can simplify life by chopping your view of it into little bits and then attending to the bits. But if you do that—and our cognitive biases lean all of us in that direction—you miss much of the reality of life, and you diminish your ability to deal with it effectively.

The best thinkers develop an instinct, a habit of mind, which enables them to integrate their thinking so that they're always aware of the entire integrated phenomenon of life and all of its manifestations.

Whole Mind Thinking

Whole mind thinking is the intentional use of both analytical thinking, which is mostly conscious and logical, and intuitive thinking, which is mostly unconscious. Most of us rely predominantly on one or the other way of thinking, analytical or intuitive. We would describe it to others with statements like "I trust the facts" or "I trust my gut."

The importance of whole mind thinking is that the whole mind is better at decision-making than either "I trust my gut" or "I trust the facts." Decisions made with whole mind thinking are far more likely to be good decisions than decisions made with only one or the other way of thinking. Also, whole mind thinking, especially intuitive thinking, helps you think outside the box, increases your creativity, and enhances your ability to see new ways of doing things and new things to do.

If your first instinct when making important decisions is to rely on your intuition—if it feels right, do it; if it doesn't feel right, don't do it—then you need to add some analysis to the decision. Run the numbers. Research the facts. Apply logic to the situation. If the analysis supports your intuition, you'll make a much better decision. If the opposite is true and your first instinct is to rely on the analytical approach, then you need also to touch base with your intuition. Did the analysis lead you to a solution that feels right? Again, if your intuition supports your analysis, you'll make the best possible decision.

The point is that your decisions will be more consistently effective if you use both analysis (conscious mind thinking) and intuition (unconscious thinking, specifically the coherence function or your unconscious mind). You won't always be right, but you'll be right a lot more than if you only trust your gut or you rely on analysis.

When your intuition and your analysis come to the same decision, that's the best you can do. When one disagrees with the other—when your analysis says "no" but your intuition says "yes" or vice versa, then you have more work to do. Research the problem. Learn everything you can about it. Develop more alternatives. Refine your assumptions. Evaluate more scenarios. Brainstorm more ideas. That will fuel both your unconscious thinking (remember WYSIATI?) and your conscious thinking. Keep it up until your intuition and your analysis support each other in that they're both saying "yes" or both saying "no." To be on the safe side, when you are not able to reconcile your analysis and your intuition, treat it as a "no." It's probably a sign that something is still incomplete or erroneous about your thought processes.

Whole mind thinking increases the scope of your thinking and applies two completely different ways of thinking to your problems and decisions. It opens you up to a much broader range of possibilities, opportunities, threats, challenges, and more ways to take action.

Creativity (Thinking Outside of the Box)

Are you creative? If you said "no," you're wrong. You are creative; we all are. We don't all make good use of our creative potential, but we all have it.

Creativity is the part of strategic thinking that enables you to come up with ideas, practices, strategies, plans, out-of-the-box thinking, business models, new processes—anything new or different from past habits and conventional thinking. It's also the part that opens you up to understanding other points of view, seeing all the possibilities in a situation, and generating a broader perspective of the world.

Creativity isn't constrained to the known and familiar. Conventional thinking and old habits mean nothing to your unconscious mind, and that's where creativity lives. Your unconscious mind is free-ranging and naturally creative unless you do something to restrain it. What is something that could restrain your natural creativity? Refer back to the habits of thinking and being that I described in the earlier chapters of this book, most importantly your cognitive biases and blocker habits. As you continue to do the work of identifying and converting your ineffective habits of mind, your creativity will naturally reassert itself, and you'll find yourself effortlessly thinking outside of the box.

You don't have to create creativity; all you have to do is set it free, and you're already doing that if you're working on your habits of mind.

There's a grander, large-scale form of creativity that I call "strategic creativity" to differentiate it from the simple creativity that's released when you get your dysfunctional habits of mind out of the way. I'll cover it in the next chapter.

Double Vision

Double vision is nothing more than the ability to see things from other points of view. Perhaps it would be better named "multivision." It's wise to see things from many points of view. Double vision keeps you from getting too narrowly focused and entrenched into a single point of view.

There are two reasons that double vision is so valuable. One is that it enables you to pay attention to both the strategic path of your life and activities and at the same time attend to their details. Too many people get immersed in the minutiae of their daily lives and neglect to come up for air and pay attention to the strategic goals and directions that really define their futures.

The other reason is that double vision helps keep you grounded in reality. Thinking that's removed from the reality of a situation—in other words, thinking that's based on a distorted or too-narrow understanding—won't be nearly as effective as reality-based thinking, and seeing as many different points of view will get you closer to that.

For instance, one form of double vision is short-term (immediate) and long-term (future) thinking. If your attention is glued to your daily grind, you can easily lose track of the big picture and stray from the strategy that will get you to your goals. On the other hand, if you don't take care of your short-term needs, you can't build a long-term future. Effective people take care of their immediate needs in ways that make sure their actions are in harmony with their long-term goals. The best results come from a mix of both points of view.

Another form of double vision—this one from business—is the customer point of view and the business point of view. You need to keep the customer's point of view in mind in order to keep them happy and generate a strong revenue stream, and at the same time, you need to attend to the business, keeping employees productive and content while also keeping costs down.

Examples of Double Vision

Long-term	Short-term
Strategic	Operational
Big-picture	Detailed
People as objects	People as individuals
Self-centered	Other-centered
Cost	Value
Intuitive	Logical
Effective	Ethical
Individual rights	Group well-being
Theoretical	Practical
Immediate impact	Future impact
Urgent	Important

Curiosity and a Hunger for Information

Strategic thinking feeds on information. Remember, the best thinkers are information junkies. It's one of the ways they stay alert for and aware of the flow of possibilities and opportunities available to them. They gather information from all kinds of sources about all kinds of things that do or could affect their futures. They're curious about everything. They notice anything and everything that has or might have anything to do with their lives.

In terms of mind science, curiosity feeds your WYSIATI and packs your unconscious thinking with the ammunition your coherence function needs to feed your conscious thinking with a more complete understanding of just about anything.

Developing Your Strategic Thinking

People who develop their strategic thinking usually do it accidentally, as a byproduct of living and responding to the pressures of life, relationships, and career. It takes time and some trial and error, because you're developing the new habits of mind, but you can accelerate the process. You can ramp up your strategic thinking quickly with fewer of the mistakes that come with trial and error using the key question method shown in the table below.

<table>
<tr><td colspan="2" align="center">Developing Your Strategic Thinking
For important decisions, plans, and goals, use these Key Questions
to stimulate and develop the five habits of strategic thinking.</td></tr>
<tr><td align="center">HABIT OF THINKING</td><td align="center">KEY QUESTIONS TO DEVELOP THE HABIT</td></tr>
<tr><td align="center">HOLISTIC THINKING</td><td>How does it all work together? …or…
Who will this decision or action affect, and how will it affect them?</td></tr>
<tr><td align="center">WHOLE MIND THINKING</td><td>Does this make sense? …<u>and</u>…
What's my "gut feeling" about this?</td></tr>
<tr><td align="center">CREATIVITY</td><td>What are other possibilities (even if they seem unlikely or unworkable)?
[For important innovation, use the Strategic Creativity Process, described in the next chapter]</td></tr>
<tr><td align="center">DOUBLE VISION</td><td>Is there another way to look at this situation or another point of view I should understand? …or…
How would others see this situation?</td></tr>
<tr><td align="center">CURIOSITY</td><td>What's the truth, the whole truth, and nothing but the truth about this situation? …or… What do I not know about this situation?</td></tr>
</table>

Ask yourself these questions every time you have an important issue, decision, plan, etc. to consider. With practice, this process will become an unconscious, automatic, and highly productive meta habit.

CHAPTER TWENTY-ONE

Strategic Creativity

Dealing with Life's Big Problems and Opportunities

The Secret to Creative Thinking

There are many levels of creativity. There's cleverness and wit, which are spontaneous instances of creativity that you don't think about; you just do. There is resourcefulness, which is the ability to figure out problems and do things that don't have easy fixes. There is artistic creativity, which is a way to translate emotions and ideas into images, words, and objects that appeal to the unconscious mind in impactful and/or novel ways. And there is strategic creativity, which finds ways to take on life's big and serious problems and opportunities. If something is important and it will make a difference in your life—an important relationship, a big risk, a major life decision—you need to think strategically and creatively about it.

If you're one of those people who don't believe they're creative, then drop that belief like a hot potato. I've said it before in this book, and I'll say it again: you are creative. Creativity is a natural part of the way your brain functions and your mind works. You may not yet know the best ways to use your creativity, or you may have smothered your creativity under your particular lifetime of conditioning and your collection of habits of mind—creativity doesn't do well in a goldfish bowl—but you are creative. It's built into you. You just have to be able to access it.

Creativity takes many forms, and the form that is most useful for building a successful life is the meta habit I call "strategic creativity."

In ways we don't fully understand, the coherence function of your unconscious mind takes in everything you perceive and all the information you gather and somehow generates insights and breakthroughs. You know the experience; we all do. You work on solving a problem or taking advantage of an opportunity, and you come up with all kinds of possible solutions, but somehow you know they're not quite right. So you turn your mind to other pursuits. Then, when you don't expect it, the solution suddenly pops into your mind. Your unconscious mind continued to work the problem while you were sleeping or doing other things, and when it came up with the solution, that solution suddenly appeared in your conscious mind. It's the well-known aha moment that we all experience from time to time.

When you dropped the problem, turned your mind to other things, or slept on it, you took a creative pause. By gathering information and consciously thinking about the problem or opportunity, you gave your unconscious mind the ammunition it needs to stimulate its creativity, but it can also need a bit of time. The creative pause puts you in a relaxed frame of mind with minimal stress, which frees the unconscious mind to make all the connections and associations it needs to be creative. This is critical because mind science has confirmed that stressful, concentrated thinking gets in the way of creativity. It's a form of the focus blindness I mentioned earlier in this book.

A caution: if you have too little information or if you fill your mind with false information, questionable assumptions, wishful thinking, and myths, the coherence function of your unconscious mind will work on it as it was designed by evolution to do, but your creativity will be consistent with those flaws rather than reality. Your creative mechanism will work great, but if you feed it bad or incomplete information, that will limit and distort your creativity. Again, garbage in, garbage out. That's one of the main reasons I had you working on your habits of mind earlier in this book, so that your conscious and unconscious thinking will be based on reality (facts) or, when facts are missing or questionable, based on reasonable assumptions or even on the very valuable frame of mind of "I don't know." Remember, "I don't know" is a lot better than false knowledge and flawed assumptions.

So the key practice for strategic creativity is first to do the information gathering and all the conscious thinking you can about the problem or opportunity and then drop it and turn your conscious mind to other things. Give your unconscious mind the creative pause it needs to come up with the answer to your problem.

The Strategic Creativity Process

Let me tell you another personal story, this time about creativity and innovation. More than two decades ago, I worked for Michael Gerber, the celebrated guru of small business entrepreneurship, whom I mentioned earlier. My responsibility was to create the E-Myth Mastery Program, which was used to teach thousands of business owners the entrepreneurial skills necessary to grow their businesses. The name E-Myth (Entrepreneurial Myth) came from his all-time best-selling book about developing an entrepreneurial mind. I was intimidated by the challenge of inventing and writing more than one hundred coaching booklets of ten to twenty-five pages each. I still remember clearly the moment I took the first booklet I wrote to Michael for his approval, thinking to myself, "Did I get it right?"

My relief was enormous when he told me that he was delighted that it was both innovative and true to his E-Myth principles. My relief was short-lived. Having broken the ice with the first booklet, my next thought was "How in the world am I going to create one hundred more of them?" Each booklet had to be innovative; something no other coaching business had. Yet each booklet had to be true to the E-Myth principles, usable by any business coach working with any small business leader in any industry and in any country. I had gotten the first one right, almost by accident as I remember. I had to come up with a systematic way to do it again—one hundred times.

Well, I did it.

Long story short: I came up with an early version of the creative process shown below. It worked. Every time. Yes, *every* time. After completing two or three more booklets using this process, my confidence soared. By the time I completed another couple of booklets, the process had become habitual, and I knew beyond a doubt that I could, without fail, every time, produce one hundred, one thousand, or any number of booklets. And later, in business and in life, when the need for innovation arose, I had a built-in habit of thinking that served me well and is still serving me well.

Like all habits, the habit of thinking creatively is established through repetition. It takes time and practice. Use the process outlined below, and stick with it. Sooner, rather than later, it becomes habitual.

The Strategic Creativity Process

1. Clearly state the issue, problem, opportunity, or innovation you want to solve. Be clear about this because clarity will focus both your conscious and unconscious thinking. Sometimes the hardest thing to do is to state the problem, opportunity, or objective.

2. Gather and study as much information as possible. Be clear about the information you gather; know what's factual, what's questionable, and what is unknown. If you include assumptions, conventional wisdom, or questionable facts, be aware of them. If you simply do not know some things, either leave them unknown or, if you absolutely have to, make reasonable assumptions. Remember, what I see as a reasonable assumption you might see as a stupid belief and vice versa.

3. Try to come up with a solution or to resolve the issue consciously with whole mind thinking. Ask others what they think. Do the research. Study the problem and turn over every stone in your search for the answer. Use brainstorming, guided fantasies, free association, and any

other techniques you know about for stimulating creativity. Exhaust all the possibilities.

4. Then take a break. Take a *creative pause* to allow your unconscious mind to continue to work on the issue. Do something completely unrelated to the problem, maybe something fun or relaxing. Sleep on it if necessary. This can be the most difficult part of the process, especially if you're a decisive, action-oriented person. It can feel lazy or irresponsible. After all, isn't work the answer to all your problems?

5. Allow the solution to emerge. You have to allow the unconscious mind to work at its own pace. If you try too hard, you create stress blindness, which disrupts and delays your unconscious thought processes.

6. When the solution or the aha moment gives you an idea, you may still have to use some conscious thinking to make it workable. Often, the answer comes in the form of an idea or impression (that's how the unconscious mind communicates with the conscious mind), and you have to put shape and practicality to it. Remember that the conscious mind is the safeguard against the occasional weirdness of the unconscious mind. The conscious mind should always be the decision-maker in matters of importance.

Most of the time, this process will result in an innovation or the best possible solution to a problem or opportunity. Now and then, you'll resolve the issue while consciously working on it; you consciously arrive at the best solution, or your unconscious mind works quickly. Occasionally, you never do arrive at a workable resolution as there may not *be* one.

This form of creativity isn't a habit of mind. It shouldn't "go unconscious" in the way that you want other habits of mind to become unconscious. But it should be habitual, meaning it should become your go-to mindset when something is important to your future.

The keys to success in strategic creativity are two things. First, make sure the WYSIATI in your head is as complete, accurate, and trustworthy as you possibly can. You can never know too much, although you can know too much if what you know (or think you know) isn't accurate or complete or depends on a flawed Reality B. Second, trust the process, and trust your unconscious mind—your coherence function—to do the job.

CHAPTER TWENTY-TWO

End Note: Master Your Mind, Master Your Life

I've made a prediction to myself about the people who read this book. I've predicted that more than half of you won't really engage in the work that I've outlined. Either you won't really believe it, you'll be too impatient, you'll cherry-pick a few ideas that seem useful, or you'll think you get it when, in fact, you don't. Your cognitive biases and personality blockers will continue to get in your way, and all the while, you'll be totally convinced that you're on top of the situation. You'll continue to believe that you long ago mastered the art/science/skill of perceiving reality as it is. You won't buy into the idea that your mind distorts things routinely, and you'll continue to believe beyond any doubt that the Reality B that lives in your mind is identical to the Reality A that occurs outside of your mind in the real world. Part of that false reality is that your conscious mind is now and always has been in charge of your life. Your me-bias and self-perceptions will tell you that you already knew all that stuff about cognitive biases and that your failures and disappointments have nothing to do with your personality. You'll sincerely continue to believe that, while others may be guilty, you certainly haven't fallen prey to any of those traps.

I've also predicted that a minority of you *will* engage in at least some of the work in this book and come to the realization that you really haven't been in charge of your own thinking for all these years, at least not consciously.

I have high expectations for this (hopefully large) minority, and they are why I wrote the book in the first place. Perhaps you're one of them. It's deeply embedded in my sense of purpose that I want this book to make a difference for as many lives as possible. I want to help as many people as I can to make the kinds of contributions to the world that can be made only by clear thinkers.

I've been purposefully repetitive about one point in this book, and that point is this: when you take on new habits of mind, at first they feel wrong, awkward, sometimes embarrassing, and oh-so-slow and unnatural. You have to engage them. You have to practice them over and over until they become innate, automatic, and unconscious. You have to consciously and conscientiously discipline yourself to make them into the new habits of thinking that they need to be. I've led you to expect that, with enough practice, each will become a new, productive habit of mind. Although that's true, there's a greater benefit.

Collectively and over time (not too much time), these new habits of mind will interrelate and integrate in both your conscious and unconscious mind until, ultimately, your goldfish bowl will fall away and clear thinking will be your new normal. That may not sound like much, but given your starting point (and mine), it's actually miraculous. When your new norm becomes clear thinking, everything opens up for you. In fact, an appropriate title for this book might have been *Clarity: Getting Reality Right*.

I want to reinforce one more idea before you close this book. As I said earlier, I don't believe in transformation except for caterpillars and tadpoles. I'm not asking you to transform into something you're not. I'm talking about authenticity. If you engage in the work I've described in these pages, you won't be transformed into somebody new; that's impossible anyway. You'll uncover the authentic you, the real you who has been buried under decades of conditioning and the sometimes tyranny of your own mind.

All I've really done with this book is give you a manual for taking control of your mind and returning to the authentic you.

I wanted to end this book with something profound, but you know what? That's for you to do. Clarifying your mind, finding ways to see reality as it actually is, seeing yourself as you really are, thinking straight when you need to…it's all up to you, and always has been.

I wish you well.

APPENDICES

APPENDIX A
Best Books for Nonscientists about Mind/ Brain Science

Thinking, Fast and Slow
Daniel Kahneman (Nobel Prize laureate)
(This is the single best book on the subject of the mind and how it behaves; if you read nothing else, read this.)
2011 ISBN: 978-0-374-27563-1

Subliminal: How Your Unconscious Mind Rules Your Behavior
Leonard Mlodinow
2012 ISBN: 978-0-307-37821-7

Incognito: The Secret Lives of the Brain
David Eagleman
2011 ISBN: 978-0-307-38992-3

Born to Believe: God, Science, and the Origin of Ordinary and Extraordinary Beliefs
Andrew Newberg and Mark Robert Waldman
2006 ISBN: 978-0-7432-7498

Blink: The Power of Thinking Without Thinking
Malcolm Gladwell
2005 ISBN: 0-316-17232-4

The Highest Goal: The Secret that Sustains You in Every Moment
Michael Ray
2004 ISBN: 1-57675-286-0

Creativity in Business
(Based on the famed Stanford University course that has revolutionized the art of success)
Michael Ray and Rochelle Myers
1986 ISBN: 0-385-24851-2

A Technique for Producing Ideas
James Webb Young
1940 (This is an old book. It predates the ISBN numbering system. You may not be able to find it.)

The Habit Factor
Martin Grunburg
2010 ISBN: 978-0982050132

Brainwashed: The Seductive Appeal of Mindless Neuroscience
Sally Satel and Scott O. Lilienfeld
2013 ISBN: 978-0-465-01877-2

The Eight-Sense Experience

Reliving and Preliving the Events of Your Life

We have five senses: sight, hearing, touch, smell, and taste. Each sense is a pathway for information to get into our minds. The five senses provide the raw material for our perceptions of what's real, our Reality B. Remember that Reality A is the actual reality that exists in the real world outside of our minds, and Reality B is our internal perception of that reality; they often are not the same.

Thoughts, emotions, and bodily sensations aren't really senses; they're mental activities that enable us to make sense of our experiences by reacting to and interpreting the information brought to us by our senses. Thoughts and emotions are familiar to all of us, but you may not have paid much attention to your bodily sensations, so let me say more about them.

The bodily sensations I'm talking about originate in our minds, but we feel them in our bodies. What do I mean by "bodily sensations"?

- The tingling that accompanies fear or anger

- The light, open feeling parents get while looking at their sleeping children

- The heavy, leaden feeling many of us get when we're dreading something

- The electric sensation we get when we're startled

- That sinking feeling in the pit of the stomach that signals tension and anxiety

- Any number of other bodily sensations we get in response to conscious and unconscious thoughts and impressions

There are other ways the mind translates conscious and unconscious thinking into the body, for instance, the movement of muscles in response to the mind's intentions. I think, "I'll pick up that spoon," and my mind unconsciously directs the right muscles to move in such a way that I pick up the spoon.

Another mind-body connection is the so-called placebo effect, in which the beliefs of the mind influence the operation of the immune system and some healing processes. There are others, and science is beginning to understand the mechanisms by which some of these mind-body phenomena work. So the fact that we have bodily sensations that originate in the mind should come as no surprise to you.

You live your life in these eight dimensions of experience, which are sight, hearing, touch, taste, and smell, plus the three interpretive functions expressed as thoughts, emotions, and bodily sensations, all of which I collectively call the eight-sense experience.

Your entire life has been and will continue to be one long, extended eight-sense experience.

So what? Why is the eight-sense experience a valuable tool in your efforts to develop useful habits of mind and to create within you the most accurate Reality B? The short answer is that the eight-sense experience allows you to become aware of your unconscious habits of mind and the triggers that set them in motion. That awareness enables your conscious mind to take charge of those habits and change the ones that aren't working for you. In other words, the eight-sense experience helps you access your unconscious thinking and gives you a way to reshape your unconscious habits of mind.

To explain, let me first remind you that your habits of mind are mostly unconscious, were mostly unconsciously developed, and are anchored to your unconscious ways of thinking, believing, and feeling. Some of them, mainly your personality habits, are deeply anchored in your earliest childhood experiences. The eight-sense experience is a way to mentally relive events in your past and, unlike mere remembering, put you in touch with the conscious and unconscious associations that occurred in the original experience. No, the reexperienced event in your mind won't be as intense or fully experienced as the original one was, but if you immerse yourself in it and bring forth as much of the eight-sense impact as you can, it'll bring back many of the stronger impressions and allow you to get access to much of the unconscious part of the original experience. It will not be all of the experience, but there will be a lot, and more than enough to give you access to and make you consciously aware of much of the unconscious workings of your habits of mind.

That's the value of the eight-sense *re*experience; it enables you to relive the disappointing events of your life in such a way that you become consciously aware of your counterproductive habits of mind, and that awareness gives you the leverage to shift them into something more productive.

An eight-sense visualization of a future experience—an eight-sense *pre*experience—gives you a way to mentally practice new habits of mind and integrate them into your ways of thinking and being. In the privacy of your own mind, you can actually use your imagination to practice new behaviors with none of the risk of failure or embarrassment that so often arises from changing a habit when you're new at it and probably clumsy and hesitant. Believe it or not, this imaginary practice changes your brain by beginning to create new connections—new brain circuitry—that, with repetition and practice, will quickly become new and improved habits of mind. In other words, you'll learn to think better and more clearly both consciously and unconsciously.

Let me summarize: An eight-sense *re*experience can enable you to mentally relive a past experience and bring much of the unconscious parts of that experience into your conscious awareness so that you can identify and understand your unproductive habits of mind. Furthermore, you can redesign your own habits of mind and use the eight-sense *pre*experience to practice new ways of thinking and being until they replace old, unproductive habits. You can actually reprogram yourself to upgrade your mind, and the eight-sense preexperience helps you do it.

Another thing to consider is triggers. Habits, including unconscious habits of mind, are bundles of neural activity that get triggered (consciously or unconsciously), automatically go into action, and run their course. An eight-sense reexperience allows you to discover your triggers at the same time you're discovering the habits they set in motion.

Why are triggers important? When you know what triggers a habit of mind, you can use that trigger as an alert, which tells you when to consciously interrupt an unproductive habit and consciously redirect your thinking and behavior into more productive thoughts and actions. In short order, you break the old habit, and a new, improved habit becomes anchored to the old trigger. You'll see what I mean below as you look more closely at the eight-sense experience.

All of that was a long way to say that the eight-sense experience—whether *reex*perience or *pre*experience—enables you to understand your unproductive habits of mind and to identify what triggers them into action.

Let me show you how it works with an example. In this case, I'll use the example of someone I'll call John, who wants to reexperience a disappointing event in his life so he can discover the unproductive habits of mind that produced the disappointment. By the way, you can have an eight-sense reexperience by yourself, but it's usually better to be coached by a trusted friend or advisor, and the example below includes John's friend Jane, who coaches him through the experience.

The process is pretty simple, although as I've said repeatedly, it'll be awkward and slow at first, like any new skill you take on. First, you choose a place and time when you won't be interrupted or distracted for about fifteen to thirty minutes, then you recall a time in your life when you were unsuccessful or when things fell significantly short of your expectations, and you mentally immerse yourself in the experience, reliving in your mind as much of the sights, sounds, smells, tastes, textures, thoughts, emotions, and bodily sensations as you are able to bring forth.

Here goes. It's a rather long tale, and it'll help if you try to get into the thinking of John and Jane without injecting your own thoughts and experiences.

Jane: *Okay, John, close your eyes and relax.*

Jane pauses while John settles in.

John: *I'm ready.*

Jane: *You said that the experience you want to explore is the time you went to your boss to ask for a pay raise but were severely criticized by him and denied the raise. Is that right?*

John: *Right.*

Jane: *To get the process started and to set the scene, think back to the moments just before you met with your boss, and quickly remember the experience from start to finish. Let me know when you're done.*

Jane waits. It takes less than a minute.

John: *Got it.*

Jane: *For the next few minutes, I'm going to prompt you to relive the details of that scene so that you'll be mentally immersed in it and as close to your original state of mind as you can get. This is the eight-sense reexperience we talked about.*

For about five minutes, Jane prompts John to recall and reexperience everything about the meeting with his boss by asking probing questions. She pauses frequently to allow John to fully reexperience the eight different kinds of impressions he experienced during the event.

> *What did your boss's voice sound like? Were there any other sounds like air-conditioning, auto traffic outside, sounds from outside his office, rustling of your or his clothing, tapping of pencils or fingers, or any other sounds?*

She pauses.

> *Were there any odors, pleasant or unpleasant?*

She pauses again.

> *Recall the feeling of your feet on the floor and your butt in the chair. Were you warm or cool? Do you remember how the chair felt, the slight pressure of your shirt collar on your neck, or the pressure of your boss's hand as you shook hands? Were there any other sensations of touch or texture?*

Jane waits.

> *Were there any tastes associated with the meeting, such as coffee or other refreshment?*

She lets John think.

> *What thoughts were going through your head as you approached your boss's door and as the meeting started? Were you worried? Were you confident or uneasy? Did you have any scenarios running through your mind? Did your thinking change as the meeting progressed?*

Jane pauses.

> *What was your emotional state? Were you anxious, happy or sad, nervous, or feeling any other emotion? Look carefully for hints of emotion that you might not have noticed at the time or that you were suppressing. Did your emotions change as you entered your boss's office and as the meeting moved along?*

She waits.

> *Did you have any bodily sensations, such as tightness anywhere, tingling, the urge to yawn, bodily heaviness or lightness, stomach uneasiness, anything around your solar plexus...anything at all, however slight, however unimportant?*

She pauses one last time.

> *Are you fully immersed in the experience?*

John: Yes.

Jane: *Okay. In the days or hours before the meeting with your boss, what were your expectations for the meeting? Not your hopes but your expectations. And how confident were you about your expectations?*

Note: This seems to interrupt the process by injecting conscious thoughts from an earlier point in time, but not only does it reactivate John's expectations, but it also allows his unconscious mind to continue to reengage with the experience of the meeting. It also helps him recall his Reality B at the time, which was certainly distorted; otherwise, the meeting would have produced the expected results.

John: I was pretty sure I'd get a pay raise and maybe even a promo-
          tion. For the past couple of months, I'd been performing well
          above the level of my coworkers, my boss seemed more posi-
          tive about me, my work brought in a lot of new customers, my
          coworkers seemed nicer to me than usual, and I felt pretty good
          about everything at work. I didn't realize it at the time, but
          reexperiencing it made me remember that I had been feeling
          more energetic in those days and in a generally good mood
          most of the time. I remember occasionally feeling a bit off when
          I first went in to the office some mornings, and sometimes I
          felt a bit down, but that happens to me now and then, and it
          wasn't anything to pay attention to.

          So, yeah, I was pretty confident, maybe a little bit nervous, but
          that happens to anybody asking his boss for a raise, doesn't it?
          My specific expectation was that my boss would agree to give
          me a raise, maybe even on the spot during the meeting, and
          that I'd get some strongly positive feedback.

Jane: So what happened?

John: My boss asked me to sit in the chair in front of his desk, and
          then he said, "You asked for this meeting, so it's your agenda,
          John. When you're done, I have some things I've been meaning
          to say to you, but let's start with your concerns. So…what's up?"

          I remember now but didn't notice it at the time that he smiled
          at me, but it was kind of a tight smile, and the energy in the
          room was slightly uncomfortable, maybe even a bit tense.

          I started off by mentioning my excellent performance over the
          past months, the fact that I had brought in a lot of new cus-
          tomers, the way my coworkers seemed more respectful of me
          these days, and how I felt like everything was going well for me.

As I talked, my boss's expression got tighter, and he went all stony-faced. It surprised me because I would have thought he'd be all smiles and would have given me a compliment or two. When I asked about the possibility of a raise in pay, he actually frowned.

That worried me, and the awkward silence that followed worried me even more. I remember thinking to myself, "What's going on? This isn't at all what I expected."

Then he shocked me. He said, "John, you have it all wrong. I'll be blunt. The fact is that you're in danger of losing your job if your attitude and your performance don't improve. That's what I planned on talking with you about."

Then he stunned me even more. He said that my performance was well below satisfactory; that the number of customers I had brought in was high but they were the wrong kinds of customers—low profit margins from their business, they were demanding and hard to deal with, and they didn't stay with us very long—and that my coworkers had been going out of their way to be nice to me because they all saw how I was floundering and they didn't want to make me feel bad. They were actually embarrassed and felt sorry for me.

He wrapped up by saying, "John, I'm bewildered that you could be so blind to your own shortcomings and poor performance and so badly misread the signs of your incompetence."

Then he said that he needed to think about the situation for a while and that he'd schedule another meeting soon to talk with me about a remedial program to get my performance up to snuff and what would happen if I didn't improve. He closed the meeting asking me to take a day off to think about how I could so badly have misunderstood the situation and to come up with some ideas to improve my performance.

Jane: How awful for you.

John: Yeah, it was really bad.

Jane: What happened afterward?

John: We met two days later. I had thought long and hard about the situation and was trying to get him to understand why he was mistaken, but he wasn't open to what I had to say. In fact, he got really angry. You know how some people just can't see reality and can't accept responsibility for their actions? That was him. It was a very short meeting, and he fired me on the spot before I could finish what I wanted to say.

I cleaned out my desk under the supervision of a security officer, left the building, and that was the last I saw of him or anyone else in the company. It was a gross injustice, and I have to admit that, even now, three years later, I'm still bitter about it.

Jane: John, you've done a good job reliving that disappointment. Our purpose is to look back at the experience to discover if any of your habits of mind contributed to the unexpectedly bad outcome. So now, while it's all still vivid in your mind, let's dig into your thinking and see what we can discover.

John: Okay.

Jane: First of all, before we start, you'd have to agree that your understanding—your Reality B—didn't match up with the situation, did it? If it had, everything would have turned out as you expected, right?

John:	*Yeah, my boss had a completely weird perception of my per-
formance, and I had no clue that he felt that way. His Reality
B was that he was disappointed in me even though I didn't de-
serve it, and my Reality B was that he and my coworkers were
pleased with my work. And as we know, Reality A, the truth of
the matter, was that my performance was pretty good.*

Jane:	*Okay, let's start with your boss's Reality B. In order to get the
most out of reliving the experience, I'm going to ask you to
become an impartial referee and look at the experience from
the point of view of somebody who was a complete stranger
who knew neither you nor your boss and who knew nothing of
the situation. You'll have to be completely neutral, and that's
not an easy task, especially when you feel that you've been
wronged. I want you to become completely objective about
your boss, as if you were a third person watching the meeting
with no prior opinions about either you or him. It means that
you have to let go of your natural me-bias for a while. Can you
do that?*

John:	*Of course I can.*

Jane:	*Don't be so quick to agree. Knowing about your me-bias and
avoiding its distortions aren't so easy. You have to become
a critic, almost as if you're finding fault with yourself. At this
point, you're sure you were right, but to truly understand the
situation and your boss's attitude, you also have to be willing to
see the opposite point of view. You don't have to believe it, but
you need to see it. Can you really do that?*

John:	*When you put it like that, maybe it's not so easy, but I'll give it a
try. I'd appreciate it if you'd help keep me on track if you see me
getting defensive.*

Jane: *Of course I will. Now remember, you're taking the point of view of a third person, observing the meeting with no previous opinions.*

John: *Okay.*

Jane: *I noticed a number of things you said that we could take a look at. Let's start with the fact that you had developed more new customers than the other employees. How did you know that was true?*

John: *We get weekly reports showing sales results for all of us. I consistently, probably more than half the time, got higher numbers of new customers than anyone else.*

Jane: *Was there anything else on that report?*

John: *Sure. It showed customer retention, customer complaints, the profitability of each customer relationship, and a demographic profile of the customers brought in by each salesperson. But the number we all looked at was the number of new customers. It's been that way at every company I've ever worked for.*

Jane: *Is there another way to look at that report?*

John: *Sure, but new customers are the key to success.*

Jane: *Didn't your boss say that the customers you brought in were— let me look at my notes—the wrong kinds of customers because they generated low profit margins from their business, were demanding, hard to deal with, and they didn't stay with you very long?*

John: *Well...yeah, but everybody knows what's really important. Bring in lots of customers and everything is great.*

Jane: *Would an unbiased third party observer agree with you?*

John: *Sure.*

Jane: *Really...?*

John: *Well...I think so...*

Jane: *Keep that in mind, and let's move on to the next point. You said that your coworkers seemed nicer to you than usual, and you felt pretty good about everything at work, but your boss said that your coworkers had been going out of their way to be nice because they all saw how you were floundering and they didn't want to make things worse for you. They were actually embarrassed and felt sorry for you.*

John: *Yeah. My boss seemed to genuinely believe what he was saying, but I knew better. He was simply wrong.*

Jane: *What would an objective observer think?*

John   *He wouldn't know what to think. He'd see both of us and know that each one of us believed his perceptions were true. It's conflicting Reality B's, isn't it? I know my view was right, but an observer wouldn't know that. He'd probably be confused and want more information.*

Jane: *What kind of information?*

John: *Well, something that showed that one point of view—one Reality B—was closer to the truth than the other.*

Jane: *What about your own experience? For instance, the signals you were getting that you didn't pay attention to. You said that you get them from time to time but don't pay much attention to them because they're not important. Remember, you said that sometimes you felt off or down when you got into the office in the morning, and you also felt nervous going into the meeting with your boss. You didn't feel that they were anything you needed to pay attention to, so you didn't look into them to figure out what caused them. Could those have been emotional signals that things were not as they seemed?*

John: *No. I get them all the time, and they don't amount to anything.*

Jane: *Remember when we talked about triggers and alerts? How the unconscious mind communicates with the conscious mind with thoughts, emotions, and bodily sensations when it is conflicted or when things don't add up? Is there a possibility of that happening to you in this experience? You don't have to believe it's true, but try to be open to the possibility.*

John: *Jane, this is pretty far-fetched, isn't it? I know what I know.*

Jane: *You may be right, but let's test it. Remember to stay in your objective point of view, observing your inner workings as if you were a third person who could read your mind. Go back to one of the times you went to the office and it felt off. Relive the off feeling fully, in the eight-sense way, and think about the feeling and what might have caused it. Talk me through your thoughts.*

John: *Okay. I'll relive a Monday morning a week or two before the meeting with my boss. The off feeling happened mostly on Mondays, I guess because it was a fresh immersion into the office atmosphere after a weekend of relaxation. I walked in the office, saying hello to everyone as I passed them on the way to my desk. They all looked up and smiled, saying something pleasant as I passed, so I dropped the off feeling and got on with my day.*

Jane: *Good. Now go back in your mind again and try to experience the facial expressions, tone of voice, choice of words of each of your coworkers, one at a time, in slow motion.*

John: *Okay, I'm doing that.*

Jane: *What are you noticing?*

John: *Nothing much.*

Jane: *What?*

John: *Well, I don't know what it is, but each of them was pleasant and friendly enough, but something about them wasn't quite right. It wasn't anything obvious, but, I don't know, something made me feel momentarily down, almost sad. It was quick and passed immediately. In fact, at the time, I didn't even notice it, but it was there.*

Am I making this up because you're asking me all these questions?

Jane: *No, you're not making anything up. It was your unconscious mind sending you subtle signals because something might really have been off, and it was not consistent with your expectations or your mental model of what should have been happening. Instead of pausing to figure out what the underlying cause was and if it was anything to be concerned about, you did what you always do, which was not pay attention to the signals and get on with your day.*

> *So while you're still immersed in the reexperience and knowing what you know now, think about what might have been causing the off sensation.*

John: *There's no way to be sure. It's all so unclear. What if I'm just making it all up, and there was nothing to it at all?*

Jane: *Do you really believe that?*

John: *No. It was real, and it was off. I just didn't pay attention to it.*

Jane: *I want you to stay with the eight-sense memory of your co-worker's faces and let the experience sink in. Just be with it for a while.*

John is quiet and thoughtful for more than a minute.

John: *Damn...*

Jane: *What?*

John: *I see it now. How could I not have seen it all along? God, how embarrassing. They were feeling sorry for me. My boss was right, and I had it all backward. I convinced myself that I was a hero, but the reality was exactly as my boss said and as my coworkers thought but didn't say.*

That was the breakthrough. John and Jane continued their discussion for quite a while after that, using the eight-sense technique to look at quite a few aspects of John's experience with his boss and a number of other experiences at other times in John's life. John discovered that he habitually distorted his perception of reality with a strong me-bias, which generated expectations that his unconscious mind confirmed (the confirmation bias) and which were reinforced with a lifelong habit of being self-referencing to the point that he unconsciously rejected the viewpoints of all others when they differed from his and cast himself as the hero in his theater of the mind.

Ultimately, this new awareness enabled John to see his me-bias and consciously allow for other possibilities. Awareness didn't eliminate his me-bias, but it gave him a more balanced way to see himself in the context of his situation at work and in life in a more objective way.

And finally, after some additional eight-sense visualization, he was able to identify the trigger that launched his self-referencing personality habit. The trigger (which he could now use as an alert, warning him to change his way of thinking) was that same off feeling that he talked about with Jane.

Ultimately, after some mental rehearsal and practice, he developed the habit of automatically seeing a broader range of possibilities and being more objective about them. He called it the habit of "openness."

Did you notice how resistant John was to any suggestion or hint that his perceptions might be wrong? He even believed that his boss was blind to the truth and unable to see things as they actually were. John wasn't really resisting the truth; in fact, he was trying hard to cooperate so that he could understand what went wrong in the session with his boss.

John sincerely believed that his view of the situation was the reality of it. It felt to him like he was defending the truth rather than clinging to his point of view. He had no inkling that his perceptions might have been wrong and that his job was in jeopardy. Internally it all felt so real, so genuine, so authentic, yet he came to realize it was all manufactured by his faulty habits of mind.

When you try to penetrate your inner workings—your unconscious habits of mind—you can expect honestly and authentically to think and feel that your point of view (your "truth") is the actual reality. You can't help it; you're built that way. We all are. That's why it's so important to be the objective observer of yourself and to consciously force yourself to acknowledge other points of view even if you believe them to be wrong. You don't have to agree with them, but you do need to understand them. The mere fact of admitting them into your awareness adds them into the mix of information available to your unconscious mind, your WYSIATI. Your unconscious mind then does its thing (the coherence function) by evaluating all the information available to it and drawing the most compelling conclusion.

In the example above, John's unconscious mind delivered a new understanding of reality in the form of an aha moment accompanied by a sense of rightness. It was an aha that surprised and dismayed him, but it also had the ring of truth. His aha was reinforced by bodily sensations that always accompany his epiphanies—a physical feeling of relief and relaxation in his chest.

Your eight-sense exploration of your disappointing experiences will differ greatly from John's, but if you fully reexperience them to bring forth all of the unconscious associations; if you are able to take an objective, third-party view of the experience; if you force yourself to understand other points of view (even if you don't believe them); if you pay attention to even the most subtle and unnoticed head, heart, and gut signals that were part of the experience; and finally, if you stay open to all the possibilities (including the ones that don't feel good or seem wrong); then your unconscious mind will process everything, and, as it was designed to do, it will come up with the right answers.

All you're really doing is getting out of your own way and letting your marvelous mind do what it was made to do.

APPENDIX C
The Repeating Question Technique

Peeling the Unconscious Onion

The repeating question technique is a way to get a deeper understanding of an idea, a meaningful event, an emotional reaction, an attitude, or any other experience. For our purposes, it's an excellent way to bring forth an understanding of what's going on in your unconscious mind.

The Technique

The process is what it says: you ask yourself a question, answer the question, then ask the same question about the answer you just gave. You continue repeating until you have a complete, conscious grasp of the experience. The process is simple but rich with possibilities for deeper understanding.

It starts with a question such as "Why was [the experience] so important, so meaningful?" You'll come up with easy, superficial answers quickly. Jot down key words to remind you of your thinking.

Then—and this is the key to getting to the heart of the matter—ask and answer the question, "Why is *that* [the reason you gave to the previous question] so important?" Again, jot down your answer(s). And do it again, again, and yet again until you reach a full understanding of the experience and its true meaning for you.

Continue drilling down with repeating questions until you sense that you have reached the heart of the matter. You'll feel it as some kind of aha moment or a feeling of relief. It might be a sense of satisfaction rather than a sense of wanting to stop or to move on to some other subject.

If you feel stumped or blocked at any level of repeating questions, that's a sign that you're unconsciously avoiding something. You'll need to break through that unconscious resistance. Push through it by continuing to ask the repeating question and, if necessary, speculating about answers that don't feel right for you but might be true of others. Again, jot down the key words/phrases. At some point, you'll have that aha, and you'll intuitively know that you've discovered what you were looking for. Occasionally, you may still find yourself blocked and unable to break through.

Sometimes, when you're blocked and can't think of an answer, it helps to use your imagination and make up an answer or give an answer that you think could be true for someone else, even if it doesn't seem true for you. Because your imagination taps into your unconscious associations, it can pull important truths from the same place your unconscious habits of mind reside. When you explore these pretend answers, try to keep your mind open to possibilities, even possibilities you don't initially think are true for you. You can surprise yourself with breakthroughs and unexpected aha moments. There's no risk because you'll know as you explore whether or not the answer is true for you and whether or not it brings forth clues that make sense to pursue. As you explore these supposedly fictitious answers, the key is to be alert for emotional responses, especially strongly positive or negative reactions.

If you experience anxiety, however faint it may be, and want to avoid further exploration of an answer, it may be a signal that it's important for you to continue that line of thought. And, of course, if you're strongly attracted to a line of thinking, you should pursue that. If the line of exploration leaves you cold and gives up no head, heart, or gut signals, it's probably a dead end. Go on to another line of inquiry.

Getting the Most from the Technique

When you select an event to examine, don't merely remember it, *reexperience* it. Use the eight-sense technique to relive it in your mind, including what happened, what you felt, and anything else you can recall about the experience like sights, sounds, tastes, smells, and sensations as well as thoughts, feelings, and emotions. Reexperience it in your mind's eye and get a sense of what made this activity so meaningful. Spend a few moments getting into the experience of the event.

Maybe you'll get to your final answer quickly; maybe it will take many repeating questions to get to it, but eventually you'll get down to a single word or short phrase that expresses the essence of why the experience was meaningful.

Example of the Repeating Questions Technique

To illustrate the use of the repeating question technique, we'll use the example of people I'll call Tom and Janet. Tom was trying to discover his Core Purpose. He chose to examine an event from his life that was particularly meaningful to him. In this event, he was the hero of a baseball game when he hit the game-winning home run. The experience still resonates in him as highly meaningful—more so than you'd expect from a mere baseball game—and provides a clue to some of his inner motivation.

Janet: *So, Tom, which life event do you want to look at?*

Tom: *Let's try the baseball homerun one, when I was in college. For some reason, that one has always stayed with me. I replay it in my head all the time, and the good feelings about it never fade.*

Janet: *Good one. Okay, let's take a minute or so to review it in your head. Relive it as much as you can. Maybe you should close your eyes to help block out distractions?*

> Janet talks Tom through an eight-sense reexperience of the baseball game and the home run, asking him to recall people, place, what the day was like, what were the sights, sounds, feeling, emotions, and thoughts...any prompts that will bring the full richness of the experience back to Tom's mind.

Tom: *Got it. I'm ready.*

Janet: *Here we go. Tom, why was this event so meaningful for you?*

Tom: *Well, I was the hero. The spotlight was on me, and I felt great!*

Janet: *And why was that so meaningful for you?*

Tom: *We were the underdogs, but we showed everyone that we could really play a great game. We were better than they thought we were.*

Janet: *Why was that so meaningful?*

Tom: *I guess because I was the guy that made it happen. I felt good about myself. I actually felt powerful and competent.*

Janet: *Again, why was that so meaningful for you?*

Tom: *Well, it just was; I can't think of anything more about it.*

Janet pauses briefly.

Janet: *Try again. Why was it so meaningful that you felt powerful and competent?*

Tom: *I can't think of anything else.*

Janet: *Try one more time. Be open to anything that comes up for you.*

Tom: *Still nothing. I'm stuck. Let's move on to something else.*

Janet: *Not just yet. Let's try a different tack. Try making something up. Use your imagination.*

Tom: *That's kind of foolish, isn't it?*

Janet: *Give it a try. What can it hurt? Make up anything.*

Tom: *Okay. This is really silly...I was making a contribution to world peace.*

Janet: *Yeah, you're right, that was silly, but stick with it anyway. Was there anything to this idea about contributing to world peace that resonates with you?*

Tom hesitates.

Tom: *Well...yeah. Something about it felt good...satisfying. Not world peace of course, that really was far-fetched. But when I said world peace, it made me think about happiness, and that made me think about my teammates' faces; they looked so happy.*

Notice the chain of associations: world peace, happiness, teammate's faces. There were undoubtedly other associations that didn't rise to Tom's conscious awareness.

Janet: *Okay, let's go with that. Why were your teammate's happy faces meaningful for you?*

Tom: *Hmm.*

Tom thinks quietly for a moment.

It felt good that I made everyone else happier and that they felt better about themselves for a while.

Janet: *And why was it so meaningful for you to make everyone else happier and feel better?*

Tom: *Because, even though it was only for a little while, everybody's life was a little bit better, and I made it happen.*

Janet: *Why was that meaningful for you?*

Tom: *It just was. I don't think we have to go any further; this feels like "it" in my gut.*

Janet: *Say it one more time to be sure.*

Tom: *This event was meaningful because I helped some people make their lives a little bit better. Yeah. That's it.*

Janet: *Let me ask you a "reality check" question before we go on to the next life event. There are different levels of needs, you know, safety and security needs, esteem needs, and some others?*

Tom: *Sure. What about them?*

Janet: *Well, maybe this event was all about social needs. Your home run made you a more important member of the team. Or maybe it was about self-esteem. You felt good about being the hero, and for a while, your self-esteem must have been sky high. What's the real bottom line for you in this event?*

Tom: *Huh...Lemme think for a second. Both of the things you said are true. My self-esteem couldn't have been higher, and never before or since, did I feel more like a central and important part of the team. But what I remember most, and what to this day still makes me feel good, is the happiness I saw in my teammates. That's where the gratification was. And that's why I picked it as a meaningful event in my life; otherwise, it was just a baseball game.*

Janet: *Good job, Tom. I wrote down key words as we were doing the repeating questions, and I circled "made their lives better" as the core idea. Let me get out a new sheet of paper for the next one. Are you ready to move on to another life event?*

This technique can be done alone or with a trusted person to coach you. If you try it on your own, don't let yourself off the hook if you stall out for a round or two of the repeating question. Use your imagination if you have to. Keep drilling down until you reach the most basic answer.

About the Author

My full name is Errol Dean Alexander. If we ever meet, please call me Alex.

My adult life started on my eighteenth birthday, the day I enlisted in the U.S. Army. I made the rank of sergeant as a nineteen-year-old tank commander in Germany, went to West Point for four years, and after graduation had a brief but successful military career, including two years in wartime Vietnam, where I earned three Bronze Stars, two Purple Hearts, and the rank of captain in the Armored Cavalry. At various times in the army, I also earned the coveted Airborne wings, qualified as an Army Ranger, was awarded the Combat Infantryman's Badge, and received a Top Secret security rating from the US government.

After military service, I made the transition into business by graduating from Harvard Business School with an MBA degree and a lot of high expectations. I started my business career as a management consultant, went into banking for a dozen years, and then went back to consulting for another ten. I have held management positions with Crocker Bank (now Wells Fargo), American Express, and the Stanford Research Institute as well as consulting projects for the likes of Charles Schwab, Monsanto, the United States Federal Reserve Bank, Fujitsu (Japan), ANZ Bank (Australia), the U.S. Army, and many startups and small businesses. My titles have included CEO (three times), SVP Corporate Development, VP Marketing, and others.

My career—and my sense of purpose in life—changed dramatically in 1995. I was fifty-five years old when I joined Michael Gerber's E-Myth Academy (now E-Myth Worldwide) and at last found my passion in the field of business coaching. While at EMW, I was responsible for the creation and writing of Gerber's E-Myth Mastery Program, at that time the world's most innovative and comprehensive small business coaching system. I also made major contributions to the creation of EMW's worldwide network of coaches. It was during this time that I first began to learn about, and in some cases inventing, many of the ideas you find in this book.

In 2000, after completing the E-Myth Mastery Program, I made the transition into academia. I continued my leading-edge research and development of business management and leadership practices while teaching strategic management, business basics, and leadership at Menlo College and Santa Clara University, both in California's Silicon Valley.

Academia wasn't real-world enough, so in 2005, I returned to the *very* real world of small business development. I recruited a team of fourteen master coaches, raised the necessary seed money, and founded the Alliance for Enterprise Leadership, Inc. (doing business as the Full Spectrum Coaching Company, initially in the USA and Australia).

My first task was to develop a completely new, up-to-the-minute, and comprehensive business coaching system, which we call the Full Spectrum Business Development Program. That task took five years to complete, but it was worth it because the Full Spectrum program, based on what our clients tell us, is the very best available today. We're also at the leading edge of business education. In cooperation with Australia's GEM International College of Business, we launched the Full Spectrum Academy, which offers an online, fully accredited diploma of business management. You can earn your diploma online at your own speed from any location and for less than a third of the cost of a conventional business diploma.

Currently, I am semiretired (don't think I'll ever fully retire). I live with my amazing wife, Ali, on the shore of a beautiful little lake in the foothills of California's Sierra Nevada Mountains. As a hobby, I write a column for our local newspaper under the banner "Y'Think?" I am the author of two other books, which you might want to take a look at:

The Entrepreneur's Edge: Entrepreneurial Thinking and the Mind/Business Connection
2016 Available at Amazon, ISBN 9780692524671

Y'Think? Essays about the Human Spirit
2021 Available at Amazon, ISBN 979-8-4659-9443-9